Dating & Sex

The Theory of Mutual Self-Destruction

VOL.1

Created & Edited
by Amir Said

Superchamp Books SB

New York

Dating & Sex:
The Theory of Mutual Self-Destruction
Volume 1
Published by Superchamp Books

A Superchamp Books First Paperback Edition

Created and Edited by Amir Said

Copyedited by Amir Ali Said

DESIGNED BY AMIR SAID

Cover, Design, and Layout by Amir Said

Print History:
April 2021: First printing.

Dating & Sex: Theory of Mutual Self-Destruction: Volume 1
/ Edited by Amir Said
1. Said, Amir 2. Dating 3. Sex
4. Relationships
I. Said, Amir;   II. Title

ISBN 978-1-64404-001-0 (Paperback)

CONTENTS

INTRODUCTION   1

Toxic Love
Kyra Wolfe   5

Twenty-Six Days
Allyson Darling   11

In Search of A Quick Fix
Jenelle Parrish   17

How I Was Cheated On In An Open Marriage...Twice
Jeana Jorgensen   21

3 Mini Agreements to Make with Your Partner
Molly Godfrey   27

The Dutch Girl Will Be My Ruin
Shane Thomas   33

Cross-generational Desire and the Fallacy of the Father
Complex
Almaz Ohene   43

Opening Things Up
Melissa Gabso   49

The Rush of Pain
Catherine Renton   55

When I'm the One Who Cheats
Douglas Moser   59

We Can't Save Each Other Again
Becca Beberaggi   65

My Dungeon Love Affair
Stephanie Parent   71

Six Years In A Sexless Relationship Meant I Had To Learn
How To Orgasm All Over Again
Hattie Gladwell   77

Love and Other Accidents
Blake Turck   83

The Joys of Dating an Older Woman
Joe Duncan   87

Ten cuidado: A Lesson in Colorism for Boricuas (...or, Why Have I Only Dated White People?)
Elena Fernández Collins   91

Weight and Dates
Lisa Levy   101

Kink-Adoring HumanBeing
Marcus K. Dowling   107

The Hoe Phase
D. Anne Tolentino   113

Karma Is A Car Crash
Alexandra Hogan   119

Never Fucking A Guy Who Has A Podcast Again
Danielle Chelosky   127

After the Third Strike, How Do We Stay Together?
Vonnie Wright   133

Make Mine A Double
Jennifer Greenberg   141

What Happened When My Boyfriend Became My Girlfriend
Suzannah Weiss   147

Panda With A Gun
Carolyn Busa   155

Life of Bi
June Moon   159

My Best Friend's Unintentional Role In my Sex Drive
Rachel Davies   165

Gay Rapunzel
Mike McClelland   169

Self-Destruction In the Name of Black Love
Aitza Burgess   175
All the Weight Is Not Yours
Jeana Jorgensen   183
Threesome
Stephanie Conway   189
No Longer Terrified to Be Myself
Wil Williams   195
Dom By Day, Sub By Night
Gina Tonic   201
The Purity Ceremony
Shayna Conde   205
The Nuclear Option
Meaghann Ande   211
How Casual Sex Turned Into A Toxic Relationship With A
White Supremacist
E. Jamar   221
Ugly Couple
CT Marie   229

ABOUT THE AUTHORS   235

ACKNOWLEDGMENTS   243

ABOUT THE EDITOR   245

INTRODUCTION

The doctrine of mutually assured destruction (MAD) is a fitting analogy and guide for dating and sex, and the types of bonds that we form from these interpersonal relationships. Why some couples stay together (or why some bonds last) and why others ultimately split up (and why some bonds crash), often speaks to self-preservation. People in relationships — serious or casual — stay in or leave those relationships based on what I like to call the theory of mutual self-destruction (TMSD).

TMSD is a bit tongue in cheek, but as an umbrella term it does serve as a pathway to help shed light on the nature of dating and sexual relationships. As a theory, TMSD can be applied to a variety of couples, including: exclusive, serious relationships, serious open relationships (ethical monogamy), casual dating, dominant/submissive relationships, friends with benefits, sex buddies, and more. To explore TMSD's effect on relationships, I created the book series *Dating & Sex: The Theory of Mutual Self-Destruction*.

In terms of human connections, there are basic needs that we have as individuals, many of which we find can only be met by individuals who *match* us. But "matching" doesn't mean finding someone identical to us, or even someone who shares our same outlook on everything. A good "match" does mean, however, someone in line with our views on love and romance and someone who shares similar sexual desires, needs, and turn-ons. Thus, the negotiations that we make, big and small, to get what we want — or to mask what we're not getting — from the romantic or strictly sexual relationships that we're in help determine the fate of our relationships.

Likewise, there are a battery of habits that we develop as individuals, and most of these habits are extensions of our own unique nature. It follows then that some of these habits make their way into, or emerge specifically within, our romantic and sexual lives. This often contributes to the raising of the stakes of our negotiations with our partners, and the resulting questions that we ask are ourselves, especially when the relationship is rocky or less fulfilling in *all* the areas that we'd like, come down to three big ones: Should we leave?, Should we stay?, or How can we make it work if we stay? These questions are rooted in avoiding (or ending) self-destruction — either of the relationship itself or ourselves.

1

Within the walls of these three existential questions, we discover the mess — the good, the bad, and the ugly effects of the actions we take. *Dating & Sex: The Theory of Mutual Self-Destruction* highlights and explores the negotiations that we make with ourselves and our partners to survive — and in some cases flourish in — our relationships. *Dating & Sex: The Theory of Mutual Self-Destruction* illuminates the good, bad, and ugly side effects of the actions we take to be happy — or at least less sad, mad, or frustrated — in our relationships. Featuring different writers from around the world, each with different romantic and sexual relations and "situations," *Dating & Sex: The Theory of Mutual Self-Destruction* is an anthology series that features a collection of essays that are powerful, unwavering, educational, charming, and always sobering.

As the creator and editor of *Dating & Sex: The Theory of Mutual Self-Destruction*, my goal was simple: Invite writers from around the world (without barring any race, ethnicity, gender, or sexual orientation) to simply write about their moments of survival, triumph, or break-even in their romantic and sexual relationships. What I hoped for was nothing more than that, but as you will see from the fine collection of writers assembled in this anthology, what I (we) got was something much more exceptional and rewarding.

Amir Said,
Creator and Editor-In-Chief,
Dating & Sex: The Theory of Mutual Self-Destruction

March 22, 2021

Toxic Love

by Kyra Wolfe

I always expected that if I was manipulated or exploited sexually, it would mean the sex was painful or horrible, and that it was my worst idea of a man doing it to me. I imagined that if a relationship was toxic, I would be itching to get out of it, looking for an escape route around every corner.

But I was wrong.

The different kinds of love that I've experienced have had the power to transgress the boundaries I had set in place for myself. The most powerful love of all was so full of toxicity that I often rationalized it with the seemingly attractive parts of the relationship. Looking back, I know exactly how those relationships can evolve and unfold. How a relationship can be dominated by control, but can be caught up in intense chemistry and be ultimately destructive.

A few years ago, I began a relationship with a beautiful, outgoing and completely different person from anybody I'd ever dated before, an older guy. I had recently come out of my first serious relationship and was looking for somebody to show me what dating and the world is really like. He had a love of adventure and exotic food; *and he also had great thighs*. I was looking for somebody to show me how fun the world could really be.

We were together for just a few months, but they were the hottest, fastest and most fiery months in my entire dating history. The sex is, still to this very day, the most wild and passionate that I've ever experienced. Having only dated one other man, this new relationship was instrumental in introducing me to different kinds of sex, the fast, the slow, the kind that is so good you knock things off the wall and the tantric sort that lasts hours. I found myself waking him up at 3am, creating soundtracks to complement our established rhythm and losing all my inhibitions. I was absolutely smitten with him.

90% of the time, we were a great match. He made me laugh and brought out a side in me that I'd never seen before. But the ugly side was quite different.

Small manipulative tendencies cropped up early on, from the demand of not using condoms and managing to assure me it was fine not to do so. To him telling me I couldn't go on dates with anybody else, and being clamorous that I must tell the world about him while I was kept hidden. At the time I only saw his behavior as romantic, I thought it meant he adored me.

I felt nothing but good about him. My eyes were permanently fixed like that love heart emoji whenever he was concerned. I was incapable of refusing any of his demands.

The earth-shattering, bed rattling sex was a constant in our relationship. I had only been in one relationship before him, and both that guy and I were virgins at the time. When it came to this relationship, he also had years of experience on me and incomparable levels of energy, passion and spontaneity.

From the back seat of a car in broad daylight to being thrown over the bannister in my parents' house as they lingered downstairs, the sex was consistently adventurous and habitually euphoric. For the first time ever, my legs reached places I didn't know possible and my lust intensified to a point I knew could never be good for me. I'd had no prior interest in hair pulling so hard it left my scalp red, or my ankles being gripped so forcibly they were left with finger-tip shaped bruises. He would push my muffled mouth into the pillow whilst he thrust against me from the side, even calling me his 'ragdoll' once. He would hold his breath to intensify his orgasms and wake me up to foreplay. When my hands weren't physically tied by him, they were metaphorically tied to his bed; I found myself unable to leave, even making myself late for classes or appointments.

Constantly arguing about his lack of commitment and my need to feel wanted, we entered into an incorrigible circle of toxicity. I questioned my worth, and became paranoid for the first time in my life. His subtle nods to controlling behavior were always disguised under his need to be independent — that he wouldn't let anybody control him, that he was a busy man. He kept me in a constant mind battle, always questioning what I was doing wrong and never knowing when he would pull one of his disappearing acts.

He promised me things, simple things like a romantic dinner or a phone call, but he almost never followed through. Not only did this make it hard for me to make plans with my own time, but I constantly felt insecure. His behavior was unpredictable — one minute he was lying next to me in bed, stroking my face and telling me how much he liked me, and the next he would vanish off the face of the earth. His responses to my anger and accusations were often just enough to justify his behavior, but kept me guessing. It was as though I always needed to earn his affection.

All of this began to slowly eat away at my mental health, riddled with anxiety. I needed to check my phone all the time, conducting daily routines of checking when he was online or rereading my last message to check for 'mistakes' that I might have made. Months of this back and forth bouncing between fear and the most natural and mind-blowing sex finally culminated in one very painful week that I remember through tears and a hazy mind that has tried to bubble wrap my feelings. A few days after meeting my family for the first time, he cut off all communication with me without warning. I spent nine restless nights awake in bed racking my brain for what I had done wrong, dreaming that I would wake up to a missed call. I felt real emotional torment and heartbreak for the first time in my life.

And then suddenly, as though a holy figure reemerging from beyond the grave, he was back as though nothing had happened. And I let him swan right back into my life. I agreed to visit him, and after arriving at his apartment, we both sat at either ends of the room with our heads in books, barely even acknowledging each other. All while I was wishing he would come and rest his hand on my leg or spoon feed me ice cream like he did on our first date. Instead, he walked towards me, flipped me over and pushed my face into the pillow. After a few minutes of rough yet distant sex, he returned to his desk without uttering one word to me.

In that moment, I knew that the raw, palpable sexual chemistry between us was our own mutual brand of heroine. The addictive nature involved in our wild sex life had the highest of highs, the painful come downs, and the even worse withdrawals. Both emotional and physical, the effects of even beginning to distance myself from him left me nauseous, irritable, panicked.

Then in one passion-fueled evening, he hit me across the face in bed. In the middle of a fiery round of sex. I felt nothing but the lingering tingle of heat upon my cheek. Days following that, he spat into my mouth while above me, something we'd never discussed and I was instantly shocked by. Weeks later while looking into my eyes, he choked me. As he tightened his grip around my neck, I tried to tap out, but he squeezed the breath out of me and everything went black.

Again, I awoke and felt nothing.

In fact, talking about these "incidents" became a bit of a funny story of mine to tell. When friends described their hilarious mishaps in the bedroom, I offered up my own emotional trauma. Nobody laughed but me.

After a few busy months for both of us in our last year of university, we decided it was no longer working. Now looking back,

I question why availability was enough for us to call it a day but our clear bitterness towards each other was not. It quickly became apparent that had things not ended, his hold over me would've destroyed me, or my emotional torment would've allowed me to destroy myself.

In the years following, I had huge problems with understanding that there can be boundaries in a relationship when you really want to be with somebody. Our intense physical attraction blurred the lines between what is acceptable and healthy and what's toxic, and even abusive.

Our relationship thrived on the chaotic friction and fighting that resulted in even more explosive sex. I accepted his less than desirable behavior in pursuit of moments of utterly fanatical pleasure, all built on foundations full of cracks.

I didn't even recognize that what happened to me physically was unacceptable until friends nudged at me to reconsider what I'd been put through. To this day I don't quite know how to balance the feelings of attraction and resentment I have towards him. It is a strange thing to try and grapple with the discovery of what has previously happened to you, when at the time you felt elated and full of pleasure. I would never label myself a victim, as what happened never affected me in the way that perhaps it should have.

If a partner is exactly who you want them to be at times, and then withdraws on other occasions, we will continue to lust after them, whether emotionally for attention or physically. Our happy brain drug dopamine thrives on the hope of being rewarded. The thirst in a toxic relationship is quenched by bursts of those happy moments, but never quite satisfied. The uncertainty of what is going to happen causes an adrenaline release. We are then stimulated by this burst of adrenaline.

Over time it became more apparent that preventing this behavior from happening in the future all boils down to awareness of tendencies and slow learning. In order for toxic relationships to be prevented, or at least less compulsive, we must remember that we are drawn to what we know, and that is why toxic behavior continues to repeatedly draw us in.

Even now, I still struggle to manage my feelings about this relationship. I occasionally find myself reaching for my phone in moments of craze and have even entertained reconnections. I have thought of him while in other relationships, comparing faultless boyfriends to him, and have deliberated what would happen if there was a second chance. I feel conflicted between how I truly feel for him, versus what I know I should be feeling towards him. I should be fixated on the pain and emotional torture he put me through, not just while together, but in the aftermath that lingered for a long time. Instead, I am yet to be released from his clutches that keep me from fully moving on. I've had to come to terms with the fact that the most toxic, self-destructive sexual relationship that I ever had was not just the most ruinous, but also the best.

Twenty-Six Days

by Allyson Darling

It happens on a plane. No one has cheated. Or lied. No one has a secret. Or is screaming. There is no shatter of glass or hearts — only the cry whispers coming from aisle ten, seats B and C (middle seat, window seat). They've upgraded us to the emergency exit row which does offer extra legroom but does not bode well for the people on this plane if there is an emergency landing in the next three hours and thirty-four minutes.

"I don't think we should date anymore," I say

Except we don't really "date." We live together. We share a bed. Every night. We have plans. To buy a hairless cat and get married at City Hall.

I'm trapped. I can't do it anymore. We've stopped having sex. Two months. My therapist says it's because I think of him and his behavior as "baby-like. And no one wants to have sex with a baby. I'm emergency-exiting us both out of this relationship whether the flight attendants like it or not. Whether we are in a confined space or not.

I want the drapes open, the windows open, the wind in, he wants them closed. I want to stand in front of the concert and be consumed, brain enveloped by acts of art and conversation. He wants to stand in the back. In silence. In stillness.

And fine. Standing in the back can be romantic. Lovers can kiss and peek into each other's eyes like little birds. I know that. But isn't the purpose of life to connect with other humans through acts of openness and tragedy? To, yes, please tell me, why did you cry in 4th grade during math class, and did your mother raise you or could she not get out of bed for five years?

The flight attendants offer drinks and pretzels. I take both. Seven pretzels in one bag. A cup of ginger ale. I try to subtly wipe my nose on the rough skin of the airplane barf bag. They definitely regret their decision to move us to this row. This is a scene. We can save no one.

Logistics and the reality of the San Francisco rental market mean we will continue to live together for twenty-six more days. We've just paid rent and he feels entitled to this — to act as a ghost of our relationship for the rest of the month.

Day 1

The plane lands (safely) without our requirement to help anyone during an emergency landing even though we've verbally committed to doing so. We order Vietnamese food to be delivered and share a car from the airport. I do not wash his dish because now we are officially roommates. Even though we share a bed and a bookshelf. He's silent, stoic, white-hot rage or devastation, I don't know which. It's worse than any open displays of emotion. I wish he'd throw Tupperware and scream a little but he goes to bed at 8 pm instead.

Day 2

I cancel our vegan subscription meal box and eat macaroni and cheese from a pot and Xanax for dinner because sometimes it's important to give yourself exactly what you want. Whether you need it or not. Whether it's good for you or not.

Day 5

His slippers are what get me. We've been avoiding each other, but ignoring inanimate objects that remind you of an ex-lover's being is harder. I leave the bathroom and there are his slippers. I walk into our room and there are his slippers.

I made him return the too-small ones he had purchased, setting the receipt on top, by the door. Thirty-day return policy — I was my mother, his mother, a ghost of anything I should be. And he did it, he returned them for the right size.

And now, they're just lying there, the fucking slippers. And all I can think about who is going to keep the duvet cover? And Cornelius, our fern? But I don't dare bring it up. I'd prefer a duvet cover to a fern any day but my preferences don't matter here. I'm the one doing the breaking and when you're the breaker you stand by and wait to see what the broken claims as their consolation prizes so that in a few years they can tell one of their female friends, one of their only friends, "at least I got the duvet cover."

I hope it's not the duvet cover.

Day 6

I could do it on the couch. Or in the pantry, I guess, but the bed is warm and the white noise machine is soothing, and I don't want our roommate to walk in on me when she fetches chips to emotionally eat in the middle of the night. So I do it here. In bed, while he sleeps six inches away from, snoring — I masturbate.

Careful not to move the bed. I'm an insomniac and it helps me sleep and I've always hated doing it in the shower — all wet and cold. And there's something about finishing and then being in a space where people get clean, like you were trying to absolve yourself of the action you just completed. Shower masturbation should be reserved for family vacations when you're stuck in the same house with eleven people for the same amount of days and privacy is last on the list of things you'd be getting that trip, right above emotional support and successful political conversations.

No, this was not one of those times. I had paid rent through the end of the month, after all.

Day 9

I attend a wedding alone. It is a three-day celebration of love and youth and group yoga and I want to die. The bride walks down the aisle to a Beyoncé song on strings. I am a twenty-nine-year-old cockblock sleeping on the floor of my friend and her boyfriend's rustic cabin, inside a sleeping bag that was last washed before I went through puberty.

It's cold at the wedding and no one is expecting it. Guests wear denim jackets over black-tie attire and I kiss a man in the meadow. He's hesitant to lie on the ground and ruin his suit, but I've already committed to ruining my dress from the start — it's cheap and stupid and I look like a baby-shower cake, with tits.

Day 13

Home.

"Is there anyone else? Is that why?" He asks me.

I tell him no but don't tell him about the dry humping in the meadow from the weekend. I also don't tell him that the thing we like most about ourselves is the thing we like least about each other.

Day 16

Cornelius is turning brown. I still water him even though he's our shared child I'd like to neglect. His furry limbs hanging from the tub, turning brown, strings of his body that lead to rotting roots. I re-fill the watering can, five times, six times after folding the shower curtain above the rod.

I wonder if he knows his dad never loved him. I wonder if his dad knows I did love him. We still sleep in the same bed, but I stay up past my bedtime every night to avoid hostel pillow talk. Of his questions of *why why why*.

Day 19

He buys me figs but doesn't close the drapes anymore. And

shouldn't he leave them open, anyway? I'm the one that wants the openness and the corners of his childhood and to understand all of the times he was told you are bad and no and felt guilt weigh down on him like fallen books.

"It's not special because you want to know these things about everyone," he told me instead of answering.

But is there any other way?

Day 22

Cornelius is alive but not thriving. We have this in common. With the drapes open I notice the treetops for the first time in this room. And you know what? It's lovely up here, above the streets, watching the trees sway.

Day 23

I officially abandon all dreams of owning a hairless cat.

Day 24

The great division of socks occurs. He insists I return all of his socks that have made their way into my drawer over the past year two years. I empty the drawer on the floor and return every Hanes sock I can find, except one. I tuck this one away in my dresser for fun. And that is terrible, I know that, but so is being punished for a thing you need to survive.

Day 26

"But who will take care of you?" He asks. That is the question that circles down and down and roots itself in my mind.

Me. *Me.*

In Search of A Quick Fix

by Jenelle Parrish

"You trying to be friends outside of this work shit?" was the question asked by my co-worker — my manager to be exact, but that's neither here nor there. I could say that I was offended by that question, knowing what he meant by it. But I wasn't. If anything, I was shocked. But I was also intrigued.

Angling his proposition, I responded with curiosity, "What you mean by friends outside of work?" I asked with a knowing smile. He smacked his lips as he exhaled the Black-and-Mild-rolled blunt smoke, "You know what I'm talking about." And I did. I just wanted him to say it. After a few exchanged looks — coated in immediate attraction but disguised as innocent flirtation — the conversation progressed and ended with a mutual understanding between one another: we both wanted sex.

I knew that starting a sexual relationship with him was unethical and unprofessional, but caring about shit like that wasn't a priority for me back then. Besides, the company and job description didn't necessarily exude professionalism. Plus, I was fresh off the heels of a relationship, heartbroken, and willing to do what I needed to do to move on. I knew that, the old saying "Getting under someone to get over someone," was the remedy for 24-year-old me.

We spent the entire summer together. We drank, we ate, had great sex, and traveled together. It was perfect for where I was at that moment in my life. However, what I didn't prepare for was the unexpected, yet surprisingly settling, feelings that started to develop between us. Granted, because we had enjoyed one another's company thus far, we didn't bother to break something that didn't need any fixing (which now, looking back, I know was a bit of a mistake). I'm not sure how it got to that point, but I remember when I realized that something more deeper than rap was happening.

Going into the situation with this person, I told myself that I wouldn't take it seriously. Protecting my heart was all I cared about. As long as I remained selfish, I wouldn't get hurt. What I had been through before this person was anything short of traumatic. I had my reasons for my self-inflicted boundaries when it came to men. I was determined to stick to the rules I set for approaching this specific relationship, no matter where it took me. After all, this was a fun fling in my eyes. I didn't care to hold the traditional prompts of a romantic relationship on a pedestal. But the relationship snowballed into full-blown dating just a few short few weeks later, and it didn't take long for me to realize that I had done precisely what I swore I would not do: fall for another man. Unbeknownst to him, he managed to sooth my jaded heart and bruised ego and fill it back up with the confidence that I had lost in my last love let down.

Things progressed between him and me. Essentially, I was back in a relationship. Whether this had been verbally established or not, we both knew it. I trusted him, though. A feeling that wasn't ideal for someone who had just got their heart broken or someone with my history. It wasn't a trust that was backed by fidelity or loyalty this time though. I didn't want to give him that

long of a rope. I trusted his word and his honesty that he guaranteed to always give me, which was all I required. Promises are meant to be broken, and although he wasn't exempt from my hesitance when it came to trusting him, he was given a pass to show me something that I had yet to be proven wrong about. Something that I had lost along the way when it came to dating and love.

I don't think that I began to notice the self-destruction that I was doing to myself until the fun stopped between us. And even then, I was so committed to me that I failed to consider him, or us for that matter. I began to project my insecurities when it came to men and dating onto him. Although I told myself that I had my feelings under control, I didn't. Mentally and emotionally, I wasn't ready to jump into anything new, but I did, in hopes of healing the way I thought was constructive. Holding on tight to keep the promise I made with myself when we first met.

It wasn't until the bad days between us that I saw him for who he was at that time in his own life. He was fresh off of heartbreak and loss, just like I was. He was going through a time in his life that required selfishness, just like me. That realization for both of us only brought on angst and a sense of urgency. We were both two emotionally unavailable people that skipped the healing process for the sake of moving forward.

Because we neglected ourselves, we both regressed and fell further into self-destruction. The leftover unattended pain that was caused before us began to seep out like poison ivy. And after a few months in comfort with one another, we both jumped back into bad habits. Sabotaging and self-serving our own needs in the name of survival of the fittest, with disappointment being the most feared result.

Disappointment breeds hurt, and that was something we both didn't sign up for. Our commitment that we made with ourselves — shielding our hearts and keeping our guards up — prevented us from the possibilities and the healing that we both needed. I know now that during our time together, I didn't practice self-love or self-care like I'd convinced myself that I had. I sped up my hurt in hopes of winning, and I denied myself the proper time and space to stop and heal. I don't even think I knew what healing looked like back then. However, I did know that to "not lose" or be defeated in the art of love and war (as I had once been), I would just have to roll with it, a "California stop" if you will.

I associated sleeping with someone new as the cure-all that would silence the real pain. All that did was prolong the healing process. We both made a decision to roll with the punches (metaphorically) that we were throwing at each other.

In reality, we both knew we had signed up for something we weren't ready for, but we were willing to take the risk. The only results you get from self-neglect and improper care is more dismay and self-inflicted bullshit. Naturally, that's what happened. Our lust-filled fling snowballed into something we didn't expect. What had begun as something to make us feel good on the surface level manifested into our mutual destruction. Two flawed and hurt people in search of a quick fix.

Our subconscious dysfunctional agreement made with one another was our bond. I could say that I regret that time in my life or that maybe I should have handled that situation differently, but I'd be lying if I did. During that time, I needed a reminder that I was wanted and valued, even if it came with a price. I needed to know that I could find happiness, fun, and desirability again, even if temporary.

How I Was Cheated On
In An Open Marriage...Twice

by Jeana Jorgensen

He'd chosen to not wear a condom, he told me. I stared at my husband – now ex – in shock. We were scheduled to leave later that day for Chicago, in the middle of a blustery winter, and suddenly this was happening.

"This" was not him having sex with a woman outside our marriage; that part was fine. "This" was him choosing to ditch the condom, thereby breaking the fluid bond (our agreement to use protection with other partners) and my trust in him.

I was in an open marriage, and I'd been cheated on. I was devastated. This also wasn't the first time.

During the drive to Chicago, I tried to explain why I was upset. I didn't think of myself as the jealous type; since discovering ethical non-monogamy in my mid-twenties, I'd leaped in and never looked back. Sometimes called open relationships or polyamory, ethical non-monogamy encompasses a variety of kinds of relationships (from group marriages to swinging to long-term partners who have other partners too). The main idea is that everyone involved gets to decide what degree of sexual and romantic exclusivity they want from one another, which is a departure from mainstream Western culture's default assumption that all sexual and romantic relationships must always be monogamous to be valid and functional. It generally takes a lot of frank and vulnerable conversations to work, but I felt like I'd overall had a good time of it, and I was confident that I'd found a life partner who was on the same page in terms of prioritizing sexual safety while being able to form connections with new people.

Why had he done it? I knew the other woman; we weren't particularly close, but then, we didn't need to be, since I trusted my partner to uphold our shared agreements. He didn't have a good answer as to why he'd decided to not wear a condom in the first place. "It just…felt right to do it," he said.

I thought of the You had one job meme, and I turned my face against the cold glass of the car window. When we arrived, we got food, and I gave the talk I was supposed to give. There was a party. We crashed at someone's house. I asked, in moments when it was just the two of us, for what I thought was a small consideration while I sorted through my feelings — that my husband not have sex with the same woman again just yet. He refused to consider the request. I crumpled up inside, feeling violated.

The only rules in consensual non-monogamy are those that the people entering into relationships choose to make. Once you toss traditional notions of sexual monogamy out, you need to evaluate what's actually important to you: if it's okay to have sex and relationships with other people, well, what is off-limits? Is falling in love with other people okay? Is the sex fine as long as it doesn't happen in your bed? Do you need to feel prioritized above others a certain degree? If so, how does that work, and how can you guarantee that you'll feel a certain way?

Most people engaged in non-monogamy have some rules around sexual health and safety; after all, STIs come with a fair amount of stigma, and not all of them are curable or treatable. We use the term "fluid bond" to mean intentionally going through the process of getting tested and ensuring that birth control is taken care of before ditching barriers during sex acts. Though again, different folks will define these things differently. If your agreement means having penis-in-vagina intercourse with your fluid-bonded partner without a condom, but using condoms with other partners, what about oral sex, or same-sex partners, or even kissing?

I prefer to be fluid-bonded with one person at a time, regardless of how many relationships I'm in at the time. It feels emotionally intimate to me in ways that are deep and a bit unsettling, and I just don't have the bandwidth for that most of the time.

Except.

Earlier in our marriage, we'd met a couple we liked and started dating. We formed what is referred to in non-monogamous circles as a quad: a four-person romantic unit, often two couples that have intermingled. For whatever reason, my husband and the woman in this couple had trouble keeping condoms on during sex (perhaps a warning sign I should've spotted), and it was suggested that since both parties in the other couple had been sterilized, we all go get tested and forgo condoms.

It worked well enough for a while. When there's an aspect of your lives that makes you a social outlier and carries some fear of judgment if others were to know it about you, it can be fun to bond with people like you and be able to socialize without risk of being ostracized or judged. The four of us hung out, shared meals, went camping, had sex.

Then the guy in the other couple started dating some folks who were in a triad (non-monogamous lingo for a three-person relation-ship). That was fine, since our agreements didn't put any restrictions on how many relationships anyone could be in, so long as they were meeting all their obligations to their existing partners.

For reasons I still don't understand, that man stopped using condoms with his new partners. To his credit, he told the existing quad before having sexual contact with any of us, so none of us were at risk of contracting anything. The trust, however, was gone. Those relationships withered.

Six months later, my husband chose not to use a condom with his new-ish partner and my world fell apart...how could this be happening again?

It's weird to realize that you've been cheated on (twice) when you thought your relationships were cheat-proof. Want to have a one-night stand? Go for it! Want to have regular sex dates with someone else? Great, have fun, just use a condom! Things that are normally evidence of cheating are often fine in open relationships, not that I claim to understand what counts as cheating to "normal" people since apparently some people get upset if their partners watch porn or form close emotional bonds with others, or whatever.

The feeling of betrayal, though, that's what I assume being cheated on feels like. The knowledge that we entered into an agreement together, and part of the reason for its existence was to keep everyone safe and healthy, and then the agreement was violated – that stings.

When the man in the quad cheated on us, it definitely hurt, but it was more of a distant anger and sadness, a betrayal tempered by the knowledge that this was not my life partner, this was a slightly more detached partner, albeit someone I cared for and trusted enough to be in a fluid bond with at that time.

When my husband cheated on me (and so soon after the quad fell apart), it felt like an extremely intimate violation. The aftermath just made things worse, with our strained conversations in between moments of socializing in a chilly Chicago winter. He didn't want to cut off sexual contact with this woman because he worried it would hurt her. She thought she might be leaving town soon, so he wanted to act as emotional support (somehow better accomplished with a penis involved?) to her while she prepared for that. The more we hashed it over, the worse it became, and she actually apologized to me for the whole thing, even though he had initiated sex without a condom without her knowledge. She'd assumed he'd donned protection as usual, only to find out later that he had not and had thus violated her boundaries as well (another red flag that I allowed to pass by, but which later informed my decision to divorce).

The whole thing was agonizing as I grieved the way my trust had been violated; I cried a lot and lost an unhealthy amount of weight. Feeling like he had acted in such a way to needlessly destroy the trust between us, when maintaining that trust was as simple as putting on a condom, was devastating. Therapy – both couples and solo – helped to some degree, but my partner always seemed unhappy that I hadn't forgiven him quickly enough, that I was slow to return to trusting him (as though there's a metric for these things?).

After some time, with me counting weeks for the appropriate incubation periods for all the STIs, he got tested and we resumed our fluid bond. We continued to form relationships with other people. We were happy sometimes, until we weren't, and then we divorced.

Why am I writing all this now? That marriage is long over, though some of the pain remains. I was only able to lean on close friends for support at the time, since as a lifelong educator I was unable to be out as ethically non-monogamous.

That changed when the university I'd taught at for seven years declined to give me a new contract in the midst of the pandemic. In the time since I finished my PhD there have been fewer and fewer full-time jobs in my field, such that I don't know if there will be a place for me in academia anymore. I don't see much point in specifically staying silent about my experiences with non-monogamy; anyone who thinks partaking in this relationship style makes me a worse scholar or teacher is relying on outdated and uninformed stereotypes, and the unemployment office surely doesn't care.

I'll admit that I'm writing about this in part for the catharsis, though it also feels sickeningly vulnerable to open up about this stuff. And I write so that people can learn a little bit about how others live and can learn that even though sexual exclusivity does not guarantee fidelity, neither does its opposite. People who want

25

to pursue their own pleasure at the expense of violating others' trust can and will find a way to do so, regardless of the relationship structures they are in.

But by the same token, people who want to navigate relationships – open or monogamous – with integrity will find ways to do so as well. Even after all the anguish of being cheated on twice in open relationships, I still am drawn to them. I love the freedom of being able to pursue multiple partners, even if I don't always find myself with the time or energy to do so.

I guard my independence fiercely, and value being able to make my own decisions about my sexuality. Yet I've also learned firsthand how much it hurts when someone ruthlessly chases the most independent option while neglecting its impact on others.

The revelations and ensuing conversations that happened five years ago that winter changed me, making it harder for me to trust but easier for me to assert my boundaries and values. I also became better at spotting telltale signs of gaslighting – as when someone tries to convince you that your emotional response to something is disproportionate or does not matter. I wish that I had a less insidious takeaway point than "gaslighting is awful and happens in intimate relationships a lot," but at least I've learned to insist that my partner(s) take my emotions seriously and not give me shit for taking too long to "get over" my feelings about a violation. I wish a lot of things had gone differently in those relationships, but here we are, and I'm doing my best to learn from the past while looking forward with a sense of optimism and adventure.

3 Mini Agreements to Make
with Your Partner
by Molly Godfrey

In all of my experience as a relationship coach, I believe we can either use relationships as a tool for wake-up, or as a vehicle to "fall asleep" into conditioning. Relationships show us who we really are. They reveal to us our patterns, where we hold back, and where we need to heal.

But we can also fall asleep in our relationships — get comfortable, complacent, simply cohabitate, and fall into society's ideas of how relationships should look but never actually live out our highest potential. Like everything, you always have a choice.

When working with clients I can always tell when they've gotten themselves into a "wake-up" relationship. There's a part of them that has remained dormant and is finally asking to be given space and get 'woken up'. They end up magnetizing the perfect partner in to facilitate this journey who may provoke them into more awareness. If that's an experience in relationship you're interested in experimenting with, here are some mini-agreements you can try out in an effort to draw out more intimacy and depth from your partner.

Express Instead of Withhold

In relationships, I trend towards avoidance and withholding. I've gotten better at expressing the truth and what's on my mind in real time, but I used to bottle everything up and then create a fight in order to finally express myself. I had a partner who was a very intuitive, sensitive man and could notice when something was going on internally with me. He'd ask "What just happened there?" or "Is there something you need to say?" His exquisite attention helped draw out what I usually kept inside because he created containment with his attention. Eventually, we developed a nightly ritual. When we got into bed, I would lay my head on his chest and he'd say "Ok, what withholds do you have for me?" Withholds, the things we don't say — the truth, love, desires, points of frustration, can cause an energetic block in our connections and eventually become resentments.

He held the pole of ensuring our relationship and connection always had the most electricity flowing through it. Sex was always better when we were completely honest with one another.

And so I'd answer him. "Ok well, it hurt my feelings when you said xyz." We'd talk and process it and he was able to feel if there was more and if so, he'd keep asking, "What else?"

What I loved most about this practice was that we were always discussing things in real time and handling places of disconnection quickly.

I often assign a similar homework assignment to my clients. They come back saying "Wow, I had no idea how many things I withheld every day from my partner."

Give it a try, for one week, agree to say one thing every day to your partner you may normally skip over or keep inside. Connection brings electricity back. Truth is potent.

Call Each Other Out When "You've Checked Out"

For a relationship to be its best, both people need to show up fully and give each other quality, present, focused attention when together. Nothing kills a mood more than a phone check or zone out and "half listen."

We can feel it, we're feeling beings.

For me, sex was a place I could easily zone or "check out"

and let my mind wander. It was always the perfect time to start making my to-do lists or plan out my week. The truth, sex, was a vulnerable place for me to stay present in. Being in my body and being present with my partner meant I had to allow someone to fully see and feel me. I'd often pop out and let my mind drift off into thought. My partner was great at catching this and we made an agreement to always let the other "call each other out" when we weren't 100% present. It required my partner to be fully present in his body and feel for when the sensation dropped. If he felt this he'd lovingly or playfully say "Molly, where'd you go? Come back!" and I'd laugh and say something like "Oh shoot I was checked out," and call myself out with no shame and then re-presence myself to the sex we were having. We always had fun with it. It was another spot of play and intimacy for us and as a result, our sex was a much deeper, connected, and intimate experience.

It can be a very expansive practice to add this into sex. Give it a try, play around with an agreement you keep that helps bring you both back to the spot of most connection together, in sex or otherwise. When you're fully dropped in with each other, electricity can freely flow and exchange again.

Agree to Stay Connected No Matter What

The last agreement we made together was in service to our commitment and the relationship. I don't think we get the full experience we're meant to have in life or in a relationship unless we give ourselves over to something all the way. Fully. Not one foot in, one foot out. Not sort-of. But fully. When we're 100% committed. When we surrender and allow ourselves to be used for a higher purpose, for a job, or offer ourselves completely to a connection and relationship — parts of us get accessed and used that otherwise may not have.

The most dangerous behavior or pattern that can happen in a relationship is "the silent withdrawal"— slowly distancing yourself and becoming apathetic. In previous relationships, something would bother me and I would retreat until my partner resentfully "came and got me" and confronted the issue. Or I would just resign that the spark had faded, let it die out completely, and move onto the next instead of handling the root problems.

An agreement we made in this relationship was that we would "stay connected no matter what." If something bothered us or we were angry at the other, we agreed that we wouldn't check out and instead we'd lean in to engage and actively process what was going on. To not disappear into isolation when something felt vulnerable or "too much" and to navigate the spot of intimacy together in our connection.

At one point in our relationship we were faced with a big investment opportunity. A lot was at stake and it would have been a life changing decision, one we needed to consider at our own paces. We both had opinions, it was stressful, there was a deadline, and other people involved. It was really difficult to navigate but we kept our promise to stay connected no matter what even in the heat of the debating, in the need for extra support and guidance, and through the entire wave of emotions that truly tested us both. There were times it felt as though the stress was derailing us, but by remaining grounded in our connection and the commitment to the relationship and each other, we made the choice that was best for both of us.

We gave ourselves space and grace to be with each other even when the words weren't perfect, when things got messy, and when we otherwise were dying to flee. Our communications sounded like "I'm upset at you, but I love you and let's talk about this when we get home," or "I'm really hurt right now, but I'm going to call some friends and talk to my coach and I'll come back with my part of what's going on for me." We were always able to communicate what was going on for us and to let the other into what our experience was so that we didn't end up disconnecting, dropping our attention from the relationship, or choosing avoidance instead.

These micro commitments signified the level of our larger commitment to each other and soothed the fear that the other might leave and that we'd be abandoned. It gave us both a baseline level of safety, that we could always express the truth and say the real thing and that the other wouldn't leave. It showed us that discomfort was ok and that intimacy was built in the trenches by getting through difficult spots together. That sometimes electricity is generated even in the downs because coming back out, together, leaves you both more connected.

When we make these small but powerful agreements with our partners a lot can open up. There's more spark and free flowing desire as well as trust, depth, and honesty. We can use all of these tools for "wake-up" to fully let all parts of us come alive. Start by agreeing to always say the thing you're holding inside instead of keeping it in, no matter what it ends up looking like, messy or not. Agree to stay checked-in and present the best you can, and to love each other even when you aren't perfect. Agree to stay connected and leaned into the relationship no matter what. Be willing to choose each other on your worst and best days, the good bad, and ugly.

There is the open invitation to use your relationships to become your most self-expressed self. Will you take it? I hope you do.

The Dutch Girl Will Be My Ruin

by Shane Thomas

Before I discuss our mutual self-destruction, here's how we met:

I was drinking wine and it was after midnight. I was slightly blotto. My wife and daughter were asleep. A young woman had sent me a Facebook request, and as I sometimes do when I'm horny, I peeked at her profile. Her info said she was from Holland, Michigan, was a widow, and had attended Oxford University. She was a young, blond, breathtaking beauty with the most spectacular ass I had ever seen. Truly an impressive can, as John Updike called it in his subversively sexual novel Couples. There were astounding photos of her playing basketball in a thong, and others where she was fully dressed but dream-lovely standing in a green field looking like a grown-up Heidi with a faraway look in her eye. Very pretty face. While she had a bombshell bod, her sexuality was understated. One photo by a window seemed to suggest the Millennium Bridge through a window — so the London part rang true. My wife and I had traveled there two years ago. Need I mention that the thong in this particular photo was so skimpy that a delicate cranny above each thigh emanated from a shaved vagina?

Perhaps because of the alcohol, I sent her a text on Messenger, extoling her beauty, saying something like, "Since you're the most alluring girl on the planet, sure, let's be friends, thanks for the thrill," etc. She got back to me right away and we started chatting. She said she was looking to meet new people. I was upfront about the fact I was married but lied when I said I was in my late 60s. I'm actually 70. She was 28. And is still 28, three months later.

Later I asked her if we could chat on Hangouts because I hadn't figured how to mute my notifications on Messenger as the messages screamed to the face on my phone. I needed this to be a

33

clandestine interaction. It turned out, she wasn't from Michigan, but, Holland, the country. 5500 miles away. By the next day, she was sending me more sexy photos, always with the same faraway look in her eye, and she said she loved me. Hm. She wasn't a widow. She apologized for the lie, but said she wrote that because guys were always after her. Not surprising. I never asked her about Oxford. Within a week, perhaps because the Netherlands have a monarchy, she was referring to herself as 'your Queen,' and me as 'her King.' And I was playing along. You'd think after a lifetime of experience with the opposite sex, I mean, consider my age (!) that I would have recognized that I didn't know how to swim in online water.

I don't know how much money I've sent her. Enough to have had sex in person or on screen with any number of people. What was the crass phrase we used in high school? But I still haven't gotten to third base. Just more and more breathtaking thongs, skimpier string bikini tops of photos which I've taken into the bathroom, propped my phone in the medicine cabinet with my wife and daughter in the next room, and brought myself to orgasm. That's not the worse part.

She says she's in love with me, and genuinely seems to mean it. I've asked her about our age difference many times. She's said over and over, age is just a number, and she doesn't care. She constantly writes, "I love you," or "I cherish you so much," or "No one will split us up, ever." Or, "All our dreams will come to realism." "I will love you forever." When I try to have sex chats with her, she says mildly, "My sexy King. Control yourself." And clearly, I've drunk the kool-aid because I've begun to fear she really means her expressions of love. Her tender chats seem to really come from the heart. Maybe she needs a father and a lover. And my next cracked thought: wouldn't it be cool to fuck this beautiful Dutch girl in person? Every day. And maybe it would be kinky to research the moon wandering the surface of her magnificent ass for the rest of my days, learn Dutch, and get an apartment in Amsterdam, bike to pot shops, and come home stoned out of my mind and kiss her lovely skin through the psychedelic night. Here are some of the Dutch phrases she has taught me:

Jij bent de enige voor mij. (You are the only one for me). Ik wil de liefde met je bedrijven (I want to make love to you). Ik ben oprecht met je mijn koning . (You are my king). Behandel me altijd als een echte koningin, mijn koning. (Always treat me like a true queen, my king). And as she's said daily in English, ad infinitum, Ik koester je zo veel. (I cherish you so much).

Now to the mutual self-destruction part.

I chat with her when I'm at the breakfast table with my wife. I chat with her in the car when my daughter runs to get take-out. I chat with her at the kitchen counter by our charging stations; I should mention, it's a galley kitchen: how do you say "tiny" in Dutch? I chat with her when my wife's back is turned. I chat with her when I'm sitting with the family in our miniscule living room by the fire. Or, if there's no fire. I chat with her where I write this, in my office, which is also the family tv room. I chat with her outside at the table under the umbrella when my wife's place-setting is at a one-quarter remove. When I'm in the Adirondack chair across from her, when we're on the couch watching tv, turned slightly away. When I'm on the throne, where I'm alone, but still. In the hallway. In the front yard. Walking to the park. When I'm emptying the cat litter. When I've taken the recycling bin to the curb. On a bike ride. At the grocery store.

In other words, everywhere. Places a person in my family could catch sight of my phone screen. I sometimes leave my phone on the breakfast table and walk to the bathroom. What if my daughter figured out how to get into my phone? What if I left Hangouts open? If the dirty, loving, tender, sentimental, angry, poetic or x-rated words I've written to this girl were to ever see the light of day, my wife and daughter would flip. I should mention, my wife is an extremely jealous type. She would be so hurt. So angry. My daughter who is only three years younger than this girl, would be furious. It would be grounds for divorce, expulsion from the family unit. Banishment. So, yes, I could lose my marriage. Lose my daughter. Lose my family. Lose my house, in the sense of getting kicked out and have to live in some cockroach-infested single room somewhere by myself, or in my Kafaesque version, wake up as a cockroach myself. I should mention that I don't really have an income of my own. I'm retired. Though I was a part-time Lecturer at a local university, I don't have a pension. I don't have savings other than those my wife contributed to before she retired. I don't have much to contribute to our joint accounts beside a tiny social security check.

What if my wife went through our accounts? What if she scrolled down our savings account to a month ago when I withdrew $200? As I write this, I realize I don't have a cover story. And as I try to think of one, my mind goes blank. What if she found a $100 missing from the market-rate account, or the travel account, or the account where we contribute monthly toward the taxes and house insurance? Or, the $80 purchase at Best Buy when I thought I had enough cash to buy an amazon gift card? What if she were to dig into the garbage and find the receipts from every grocery store that will give me cash-back during the pandemic? What if she asked where all the $40s or $60s went that I've saved in my wallet to go buy the goddamn gift cards? Once, when I first starting to text her the claim codes of gift cards, I was in a sketchy neighborhood picking up Thai food for the family. I found myself studying some spiky street people flirting with one another in front of a laundromat. I must have left the scratched back of a gift card in view on the passenger seat while I ran to get the food. Within minutes, that card's claim code had been snatched using a simple phone camera. The guile. The ingenuity of the desperate. In fact, maybe the Dutch girl is desperate, maybe she's a grifter. Maybe she's not even a she. I've asked her many times to text me a selfie right at that moment. She always has. But she's been terribly hurt afterwards, and I so I've had to comfort her.

Still, I have doubts. She has told me so many stories that just don't add up. When I asked if we could do sexy stuff with each other on camera, she said no, her parents are really strict and had installed SCTV in her bedroom. Okay, if you've watched British mysteries, SCTV are the cameras installed all over Great Britain! I mean, in her bedroom? Then there was the time she said she wanted an Apple watch. So, I saved up my cash-back, and sent her enough to buy one. I asked if she could text me a photo of it, and she did. It was white, feminine, and slim, draped across a gray ottoman. The next day she asked me if I would send her money for another watch—her mother had taken hers. Her mother stole her watch?! Made no sense. When I finally did send her enough for another watch, she got testy when I asked if she'd text a picture of it, suggesting that I didn't trust her. When she did text the photo, it was clearly lifted from a commercial photo, and in a bulky style that didn't seem like her taste. I demanded she send me a selfie or her wearing it. She said she was having menstrual pain, and promised to do it the next day, complaining about a lack of trust. The next day she texted me a photo of herself in profile, wearing a sexy black one-piece. On her right arm was that same watch, but clearly it had been digitally inserted there. I texted that I thought the photo was digitally enhanced. I said I didn't care what she did with the money—but why did she have to tell stories?

She said, "What stories, my love?"

What really scares me, is I that fanaticize that we'll actually meet some day. And she claims she has an uncle in Long Beach, a city 24 miles down the freeway. And that she's really coming. Here's a recent chat verbatim:

She: I want to be looking so beautiful for you.

Me: I wish I could see a picture of you

She: Yes
(She sends full-length rear-view of her standing in a doorway, wearing a shiny green thong and string brassiere)

Me: Omg. I want to kiss your magnificent ass. So lovely. So perfect.
May I kiss it? Right now?

She: Awnn. Yes. All for you. Honey, I want to get pain medicine.

Me: You should have that in the house.

She: I don't have it. I finished the last time I had menstrua tion pains.

Me: You should always have it

She: This just start newly. Do it for your Queen okay. Sees as my ass fresh. You like it right.

Me: Your ass is the most beautiful ass ever. But...As I explained yesterday, I just sent you $200. I can't   send you anymore right now. You know this.

She: Okay my love I will have to be little patience. You will enjoy my ass one day okay. You are my only king.

Me: Darling, I can't send you money tomorrow either. No matter how gorgeous your ass is. And it is gorgeous. Utterly

She: I know I will have patient okay. I understand Honey. Send me your new picture. It's been long you send me your picture last

Me: All my clothes are on.

She: What
Me: It's boring

She: What's boring
Me: My picture

She: Send okay
Me: My ass is not showing

She: I love you for who you are Okay
I don't care what anyone say about you

Me: Also, my ass is not nearly as beautiful
As yours

She: I love you only seeing your face make me happy
I understand.
I want to see your face not ass or whatever

Me: For you, beautiful girl
(I send photo of me in my bathrobe in the bathroom mirror).

She: Wow
You look so handsome

Stunning
Captivating

Me: You think so?
Thanks
She: Yes

Me: You're very kind

She: You are the most handsome man in (American flag emoji)

Me: Haha

She: Yes

Me: Perhaps you exaggerate Darling
I look pretty good for my age

She: You look spectacular for your age
Yes The love of my life

Me: I looked at your picture again.
Your hair is getting so long

She: Yes

Me: Pretty soon it will be down to your sweet ass

She: Awnn Sexy king

Me: Would you ever grow
your hair that long?
She: Let's watch and see how it grows

Me: Haha
Flirt You're really good at this, ___
You've got me by the balls

She: Smiles
Really

Me: Every time I try to pull away, I fall for you all over again
It's crazy

She: We are meant to be together
I wish
Nothing is gonna split us apart

Me: So you keep saying

She: You will be in my heart forever

Me: Same here beautiful ___
Always

She: Thanks for being there for me
I appreciate
Your love is endless
You are my king forever
Sending hugs and kisses

Me: Kiss you again and again
Kiss you beyond this life
Forever
She: Awnnn
Me: Kiss

Whether she comes or not, I'm afraid I'm going to get caught: destroy my marriage, break her heart, if she's real, or break my wife's heart, or break my own. What if I end up alone with no income and a 28-year-old to support? What if I get caught, kicked out of the house, and all our friends stop speaking to me? Surely this is mutually assured destruction at its finest. It dawned on me that for me to end up with this girl, my wife has to die. Then I thought, do I want my wife to die? No, I love my wife. But if my wife died prematurely, would I be somehow partially responsible? Had I not wished it into reality? Had I not fantasized?

Did I not make it happen?

Cross-generational Desire and the Fallacy of the Father Complex

by Almaz Ohene

What's the adjective for 'hooking-up-with-a-hot-man-and-his-pal-on-a-Friday-night-and-then-finally-sleeping-with-your-long time-girl-crush-the-following-week'?

I'm that.
Sexually fluid. Consensually non-monogamous. And proud.

One of my many sexual partners was a man I met at a literary event. The attraction between us was immediate. I was 24. He was 50 and divorced. My heart leapt when I got a notification later that evening to say that he'd followed me on Twitter. We chatted online often. A year went by and we bumped into each other again. Predictably, he was greyer than before. This time round, he asked me out.

We dated.

The chemistry was sizzlin'. The fact that he was more than double my age felt entirely irrelevant – but also, conceptually, quite hot. When it became obvious that we were going to sleep together, he looked me dead in the eye and said, "You're dying to see my naked body, right?" I nodded.

Typing those words back to myself, all these years later, they now look incredibly sleazy, written out on the page like that. But, honestly, I remember being so turned on, knowing that I was about to see an older body up close.

An older man's body is not something we come across often enough. While we may obsess about sex in contemporary popular

43

culture, virtually all sex in the media lead us to believe that sex is only for the young. The dalliance described above, which I member with much fondness, hasn't been my only foray in cross-generational sexual relationships, and over the years I've notched up an ever-increasing number of older lovers. This fascinates most people. And I'm often asked to describe the physical aspects of the sexual experiences I've had with older men, compared to that of younger partners. Of course, like anything, there are pros and cons:

Embarking on sexual adventures with much older men — pros vs. cons:

Thumbs Up	Thumbs Down
Less inhibited	Less willing to be taught new things about cis women's bodies
Less performative	Less likely to have explored sexual fluidity
Less goal-orientated	Less stamina
Less expectant	Less mobile
More sure of what they're into	More likely to experience erectile dysfunction

My penchant for making myself available to much older men has been embedded into my psyche by the Hollywood industrial complex and its ubiquitous marketing of 'Hollywood Hunks.' In the late '90s – before I was 10 years old – I already had crushes on Leonardo Di Caprio (born 1974), Brad Pitt (born 1963), and George Clooney (born 1961), due to the constant media messaging around their desirability. And then a little later, when I discovered that sex appeal wasn't just confined to Caucasian Americans, Mekhi Phifer (born 1974), Naveen Andrews (born 1969), Daniel Dae Kim (born 1968) and Keanu Reeves (born 1964), populated many of my daydreams – and masturbatory fantasies – too.

Proximity is access and the public figures we first admit to lusting after are prescribed by societal norms. Critically engaging with popular culture is a sure-fire method of proving that youngster's thirst over whoever is put in front us and that our formative crushes are somewhat dichotomously performative, yet also intrinsically linked to the key tenets of our sexual preferences as adults.

For those such as myself, who chose to date outside of the arbitrarily prescribed generational cohort, societal norms dictate that our sexual preferences must be pathologised, so the Father Complex – the Freudian/Jungian psychoanalytical term for strong unconscious impulses, usually negative, which specifically pertains to the image or archetype of the father – is mapped onto each and every partner who happens to fall above the 'double-your-age-minus-seven' rule.

As such, I've always been pretty cagey when it comes to divulging the ages of the people I date to my wider social network, with family and friends having to make do with my response, "Oh, a bit older", over and over. I'm very aware that sharing my personal experiences for titillation could be seen as trivialising the very real problems of grooming, power imbalance and coercion. There's a very good reason why we have an 'of age' of consent. However, what never ceases to fascinate me is that the age of consent varies around the world. In France it's 15; Germany, 14; Ireland, 17; South Korea, 20; in the UK it's 16 (or 18, if the other person is in a position of trust or authority), and in the US it's set on a state-by-state basis, ranging from 16 to 18.

Essentially 'the age of consent' is absolutely arbitrary.

***

I've always derided the perceived cultural superiority of monogamy and the nuclear family as the most staggeringly unimaginative frameworks in which we can enjoy sexual intimacy. And, collectively, we need to acknowledge, respect and nurture all the other ways we can physically relate to one another as legitimate rather than 'alternative'.

I'm sexually fluid, consensually non-monogamous, and proud. I seek out similarly explorative partners to discover new sensuous experiences – a shared erotic perspective can be endlessly invigorating. For example, teaching one another about all our desires has allowed me to lean into my vulnerability and build trust. And I've learned that vocalising my physical boundaries early on ensures that they're always respected.

Nonetheless, in my experience cis-het men of the Boomer and Gen X cohorts have difficulty in comprehending that women who chose to seek intimate relationships with them, no matter how casual, still deserve to be treated with plenty of respect, and not simply as a sexual plaything. I've unwittingly found myself in the latter position far too many times, often not being aware of this until long after I'd stopped seeing him. Protecting myself from the truth. But the sting of realisation always hurt no matter how much I tried to shrug it off.

Sadly, the older men I dated during this fraught era of COVID-19, were unable to have honest and open conversations about what they wanted out of the physical relationship we shared, nor where they saw it going. This could, in part, have been the emotional manifestations of attempts at self-perseveration in these traumatic and grief-stricken times.

Older cis-het men are not renowned for their ability to clearly communicate emotional wellbeing. And, during the pandemic, I had let ever increasing touch deprivation and desperation for sexual contact eclipse my usually astute judgement. In accepting highly problematic communication styles in my partners, I was continually inviting behaviours that were far less than I deserved. The subtle and predictable segues from engaging and regular conversations to only getting in touch to float the idea of a sex date, became all too familiar. This kind of nonchalance began to erode my self-respect and clouded my ability to see toxic emotional traits, until the build-up of unanswered texts I'd sent made me seem desperate and deluded.

I wasn't acting like I deserved better, and so I never saw basic decency nor honesty. But I was so wrapped up in defining my own sexuality and lifestyle choice – expecting my lovers to simply understand that this is the way I am – that I wasn't able to acknowledge my own reluctance to address my own deep-seated feelings of inferiority and abject fear of rejection.

We need to foster a culture where the bar isn't nearly as low – even in the most casual of dalliances we should be able to confidently bring our full and authentic selves to the experience, without feeling trepidation around being perceived as emotionally needy, when simply allowing space for vulnerability.

If you show up as true self to every sexual experience, you also draw out a much more authentic and uncensored version of your partners, too.

To avoid self-destruction, I'm vigorously reaffirming the cognition the only way I can be in a sexually and emotionally fulfilling relationship is by truly believing that, yes, I am worthy of someone great. And by acknowledging that the Father Complex, which, although I'd sworn it off as a duplicitous fallacy, might actually bear some truth.

Opening Things Up

by Melissa Gabso

It's been almost three months since I discovered my husband's cheating. Three and a half years of it, some of it in our house, some of it without protection.

We had been monogamous, or so I thought, for sixteen years.

When people used to tell me about how devastating infidelity could be, and what measures to take to prevent it, I took their advice with a grain of salt. Such betrayal would certainly feel crushing, I knew, but surely it could be managed.

But back in September, when a stranger reached out proffering a veritable photo album of incriminating screenshots - a Tinder profile showcasing my husband's smiling face, in which he claimed he was "slightly married," a series of graphic sexual text messages, and time logs of hour-long phone conversations - I realized that these earlier claims weren't exaggerated or relegated to a sensitive few. The knot twisting in my stomach proved their validity. I careened through a type of grief, as if the person I thought my husband was had died. As if, in fact, a part of me had died. What remained was now being dragged, kicking and screaming, through an existential metamorphosis into something new and unknown.

At first, I thought divorce was the only option. Once a cheater, always a cheater, the adage looped in my head, along with the imagined porno film of what my husband had done. I couldn't sleep; I could barely eat. I lost weight. The walk to the STD testing clinic felt like a funeral march. And through it all, that horrible movie kept playing on repeat, torturing me with all the visuals and sounds and smells that I imagined had occurred in his adulterous moments. In a frenzy of despair, I banished a couch - the couch of sin, I facetiously called it - onto a truck-bound journey from which I gratefully knew I would never see it again.

I was destroyed, and could not fathom myself recovering.

The idea of separation seemed foregone, logical, natural even. But extensive therapy and time with thoughtful, open minded friends (some of whom possess decidedly unorthodox relationship arrangements) slowly nudged me out of my misery. I began to tentatively question the ideologies I had been acculturated into, and to wonder about the very nature of sex and love and relationships. The notion dawned on me that perhaps some of the pain I was feeling stemmed from a preventable social malady rather than abject personal failure. Maybe, to a certain degree, our institutions had misunderstood love, and taught it to us all wrong.

What if the lack of respect that made infidelity so agonizing was less about sex and more about dishonesty? If honesty could be achieved and mutually maintained, then, could my husband and I develop a level of empathy that would allow for more sexual freedom without damaging the partnership? Could we think past the societal taboo of sex outside of marriage and discover a truer definition of love? Was there a third viable path, hidden alongside divorce and forced monogamy?

My husband and I had talked about opening up our relationship nearly a decade ago, back before we got married. It had been my idea at the time, and he had nixed it over concerns that I would have much more success at the endeavor than him. I now understand that his worry was rooted in the kind of abandonment fear that fuels jealousy and a tit for tat mindset. The kind of visceral half-conscious terror that, when left unexplored, upholds institutions like monogamous marriage and vilifies other ways of living.

It's a kind of fear that's baked into our society, and that's reinforced upon each of us with the overrepresentation of monogamous romance we see in life and in fictional narratives. Even the idea of a couple, as synonymous to a relationship, signifies that the only ethical partnership exists in pairs of two. And yet in modern society, there are so many examples of successful throuples and open arrangements, and so many more examples of failed monogamies, many of which fell apart solely due to cheating, lacking other toxic dynamics.

So in the wake of my husband's infidelity and the philosophical renaissance it catalyzed in me, I found myself at a crossroads, wracked by cognitive dissonance. I understood intellectually that ethical non-monogamy was perhaps a truer expression of love than traditional monogamy, but emotionally I was still bound to the traditions into which I was raised. Disney princesses. Happily ever afters. All or nothing. Good or evil. Black or white. I felt that familiar fear of abandonment - of being replaced - clawing at me.

But my husband said he needed this to feel whole. He was sincerely sorry for what he had done, and claimed he could be monogamous now, but would not be truly happy. He could also be safely, honestly, and ethically non-monogamous, if I would allow it. He was willing to do the necessary work to address the dishonest parts of himself, he claimed, in order to enter this new chapter from a place of trust and respect.

I could feel the alluring tug of potential new romances too; I understood where he was coming from. I decided to give non-monogamy a try, with the understanding that I could end it if other toxic aspects of our relationship - unexplored resentments, dishonesty, bullying - remained unresolved and rendered things too fraught. He had a history of destructive angry outbursts, after all, and I had a history of major depressive episodes. If we couldn't tackle our personal demons through therapy and introspection, we couldn't hope to bring additional people into our relationship in a healthy way.

We sat down together and wrote a list of guidelines unique to our situation, some of them hard rules - like use protection and no established friends or family - and some softer; more malleable but requiring open conversation. We agreed at the outset that we would remain each other's primary partner, and though we would still be capable of developing deep, meaningful connections with other partners, the main purpose of opening things up would be for friendship and sex. We knew the only way we could successfully navigate the ocean of gray we were introducing into the black and white narrative of our traditional marriage was through radical honesty and compassion. We needed to be able to sit with and articulate our emotions without becoming blinded by jealousy, depression, or anger.

We continued couples therapy under the banner of our new plan. My husband began individual therapy in order to process the resentments and emotional regulation issues that had driven him to cheat in the first place. And as we started dipping our toes into dating, I embarked on a journey of self-discovery that made me feel more alive than I had in years - in all of the joyous and terrible ways one might imagine. I felt the elation of attachment and the dejection of it not being reciprocated. I was let down, and had to let others down, and learn to be content with both. I learned - and am learning - about new people, with interests and life stories vastly different from my own. In meeting with others in an atmosphere of such complete emotional openness, interpersonal barriers I once thought immutable seemed to fall away. I've forged deep connections, some of which, with luck, could endure for a long time, even after changing circumstances eliminate physical intimacy.

I feel those barriers falling away between my husband and myself too. Jealousy and fear have posed their threats, and have made some days unbearable, but overall the experience thus far has been one of reconciliation rather than division. We're gradually learning to talk more candidly and empathetically about our feelings and experiences, to work through past and present traumas, and to see the other in ourselves. Three months ago, I never would have imagined that I could feel truly happy that my husband had a nice date with another woman, just as he now has the capacity to feel happy for me when I enjoy time with other men. We talk frankly about our experiences, about what worked and what didn't, and though at times there's still jealousy, we have an emotional toolkit to work through it healthfully.

I'm learning about myself as well, and have developed a sense of confidence and self-contentment that I never before thought possible. My obsessive need for self-care that I had been clinging to for years as a coping mechanism for anxiety and self-loathing is finally, bit by bit, transforming into self-love. In experiencing sex and intimacy outside of my marriage, I'm becoming a freer, more actualized sexual being. I feel more comfortable physically exploring and being vulnerable, and am able to bring what I've learned back into the proverbial marriage bed to strengthen our primary bond. Through the compassionate eyes of others, both new lovers and old friends, I see now that I have value, and am on the cusp of no longer needing that external validation to know my worth.

And for those who aren't compassionate? (Dating apps possess their fair share of selfishness and manipulation, after all.) The more I know myself, the more I know which red flags are stop signs. With safety as the number one priority, I'm developing the ability to vet people, and to see the inherent beauty and collaborative growth potential in each person I decide to meet.

Perhaps most beautifully, though, I'm remembering the gratitude and love that drove me to marry my husband in the first place. More and more, we're returning from our individual sexual experiences with a newfound appreciation for, and desire to be with, one another. In its finest moments, this experience has been a reminder, to both of us, to not take each other for granted, a notion that I would have thought counterintuitive before living it.

Will things between my husband and I progress into the mutually empathetic utopia I imagine? Only time will tell. One or both of us could prove emotionally unfit to sustain an open arrangement and our experiment could fail. And there are sure to be bumps, some jarring, even if we succeed. I still have moments when I think I ought to consider separation as an act of self-preservation; when I wonder if the mental load of our new arrangement destroys more than it builds. Inevitably, though, those darker moments are followed by the conviction that the true act of self-preservation is to maintain courage in the pursuit of happiness; to follow whatever paths, no matter how unorthodox, lead to that place of self-actualization. And for now, at least, the most promising path involves walking with my husband, side by side.

The Rush of Pain

by Catherine Renton

I remember the first time I felt something other than numb grief following the death of my mother. I was in bed with "Chris," a guy I'd been dating casually, and he spanked me hard on the ass, without warning. The rush of pain and pleasure awakened something in me. I asked him to smack me harder, and I shrieked, ecstatic to finally feel something, even if it was just pain. Little did I know that a simple slap would trigger a fixation that saw me risk my job, my safety, and even my life.

Turned on, I asked Chris to smack me and throw me around. He seemed eager at first, but when I asked him to slap me across the face, he said, "I respect you too much for that." Turned off, I quickly left his apartment and vowed never to see him again.

For a while, I'd been using sex to escape the stress and mundanities of life, but after that night, I actively pursued men who enjoyed domination, humiliation, and inflicting pain. On dating apps, I frantically swiped right and would open conversations with: "Tell me your darkest sexual fantasy, I will pass no judgment." Men flooded my inbox with dreams of choking, biting, and pain that made me tingle all over.

I met "Rob," who was in town for one night, an hour after we matched on Tinder. When his first message said, "You look like a girl who needs to be punished," I couldn't call a cab to his hotel fast enough. When he opened the hotel room door, I unbuttoned my coat to reveal nothing but a bra and lace panties underneath. He pushed me to the ground, grabbed my hair, and dragged me across the cheap hotel carpet towards the bed. The harder he squeezed, pressed, or pulled at me, the louder I moaned.

When he ripped off my flimsy panties and stuffed them in my mouth, I knew I was in for a good time. Bent over the bed, with my face buried in the covers, I heard him unbuckle his belt and knew instinctively that he was going to whack me with it. The first thwack of the belt across my ass hit me like a jolt of electricity. I screamed into the covers, not only because it hurt but because I wanted more.

Rob spent the next half hour fucking me from every angle, repositioning limbs and yanking me around like a ragdoll. I was clawed, bitten, and bruised, but I loved every minute. We didn't speak a word to each other, just exchanging looks and moans of pleasure. When he came, I grabbed my coat and left. I wasn't interested in pillow talk; he'd given me everything I needed.

The next morning, I stood in front of my full-length mirror and examined Rob's handiwork. I ran my hands over carpet burns, fresh scratches, and the red belt marks that felt warm to the touch. I took pictures, scared that when the wounds healed, I would forget the sensation. I started an unintentional Pinterest board of pain on my camera roll that I could show future partners. This is what I like and need you to replicate.

I spent hours on dating apps scoping out potential partners. I flirted aggressively, sending nudes almost immediately. Looks weren't important; I just needed someone comfortable using me as a human sex doll, who'd push through my pain threshold with minimal concern for my wellbeing. I'd been sexually submissive in the past, but this was different; I knew what I wanted – annihilation – and I wasn't afraid to ask for it.

My obsession with chasing that pain high made me call in sick to work whenever an offer of sex came up. I even faked a migraine and walked out of the office in the middle of the day to have anal sex in a stranger's car. When I did make it to work, I was distracted continuously as I relived my exploits in flashbacks when I brushed my raw, bruised body against a hard surface. My boss scheduled meetings to talk about my frequent absences, but I played the grief card. I didn't care about work and thought if I did get fired, at least I'd have more time to devote to fucking.

The next few months were a blur of names and faces I never bothered to learn. Some experiences were utterly forgettable, like the guys who loved to talk dirty but were too timid to deliver anything more than a light slap. Sometimes I could sense that the guy was thinking, "Wait, am I really hurting her?" I regularly put myself in vulnerable situations with little care for my welfare and didn't tell a soul what I was doing or where I was disappearing to, for fear they would judge me or ask me to stop.

One time, after I took a taxi to a guy's house in the middle of the night to hook up, I bumped into his flatmate on the way out. He'd been watching through the slightly open bedroom door and wondered if he could "get some." It turned me on knowing that we'd been watched, and I followed him to his bedroom, bending over and offering myself up. He grabbed my hair and yanked me over to the wall, which he bashed my head against. I was temporarily stunned but let him do his thing. The sex was over in minutes; the flash of violence turned him on so much that he came almost immediately.

You'd think the threat of real danger or unemployment would have stopped me, but it took a while to realize that rough sex was a means of physically manifesting my inner pain, the sexual version of cutting. I had a history of compulsive behavior with alcohol, food, and spending, and this time my drug of choice was men. But as I saw it, I was only hurting myself, so I pushed any uneasy feelings to the back of my mind.

It was another slap that eventually broke the spell I was under. This one was to my face, to rouse me after I'd passed out during an overenthusiastic choking. As I gasped for air, disoriented and scared, I burst into tears. It was the first time I understood this obsession with physical pain could kill me. The guy who'd pushed me too far, at my own begging, was fiercely apologetic and offered to drive me to the hospital, but I declined. I gathered my belongings and rushed home, where I spent the night sobbing.

The next day I deleted all the dating apps off my phone and looked for a therapist. It was time to end the long-term abusive relationship with myself.

Recovery from any kind of addiction or obsession rarely follows a linear pattern, it's more of a chaotic squiggle, and I had some slip-ups along the way. I can go from zero to "choke me daddy" in about a minute. There will always be a part of me that's drawn to darkness, but rather than avoid my emotions, I attempt to face them head-on. Life is tough and messy and exhausting, but it's even harder when you spend all your energy running from your feelings.

When I'm the One Who Cheats

by Douglas Moser

This isn't the first time it happened, of course. And it isn't anything that I take personally, torment myself with the ramifications through days and nights of worry. But it happens. Again.

We've had an exciting day, an opening of a show, a little get together with the cast and crew after. High on tequila and adrenaline, I whip off my clothes and crawl into bed and right on top of Andy. It's time to celebrate. I'm horny like a teenager, like the old days when sleep could wait. We kiss, me more passionately, more ready to take it to the next level. Andy is game, despite the fact that he is tired, exhausted actually. My amorous ministrations compel me to go further, reach toward what I hoped was the inevitable.

But Andy has to sleep. It is my job to understand that. His kisses soften, his hugs become cuddles. His purrs of satisfaction slip into the limpid humming of sleep.

As the house settles into the quiet summer night, the crickets and peepers giving way to the rustle of the leaves in the breeze, sleep remains elusive.

I crawl out of bed, ignoring the complaints of our cat stationed at our feet. I snatch my phone, creep into the sitting room, and spread out on the daybed, naked. The air conditioning feels cool against my skin, so I pull a blanket over my toes, rearranging the pillows so I can lie on my side like a pasha. My evening adventure continues.

I tap the app for Scruff, a hook-up site for older (and often furrier) gay men. We signed up for it as a lark, eager to sample the world we now live in, where technology replaces human interaction. It's Facebook, with full-frontal. In a moment the screen is filled with images of available men, or so they say, just miles from my home. A few more clicks and I can narrow the field to display men closer to my age, or looking for men my age, all with beseeching smiles, and alluring glints in their eyes.

Graybeard is just two miles away. I text "Hey" to him and wait. Then CTMan4Man, and Exploring, and DJ— each the same message. "Hey" I say to them. "Hey" I'm out here, as if I'm a hitchhiker on a dark, desolate highway. Any passing car will do.

This isn't the first time I've slipped out of my bed to surf my phone for eligible men, nor will it be the last. The frequency has been steadily increasing over the past years, as Andy's treatments for prostate cancer move forward, first lowering his libido, now switching off his testosterone completely.

I am just window-shopping, seeing what might be on offer from local merchants, gazing at the products, examining the wares. It's a smorgasbord out there. Men willing to show me things, sharing pictures and fantasies. Upturned asses and upraised dicks parade across the screen. Mouths smile in anticipation, licking lips, hoping to portray lust, desirability.

Earlier in the week Andy and I had a "date night." We stayed in, vaped some marijuana, drank some tequila. No TV, no big meal, just us, celebrating our home, each other. It usually starts out with music, silliness, and eventually, bed. For a couple of old guys, we haven't done so poorly. We've held these nights precious for years now, ever since we'd moved into this dream house Andy designed for us. We set parameters, just how much of the real world can we let in during one of these dates, just how far off the track can we allow ourselves to get beyond celebrating our love for each other?

This encounter, like so many before it, had a bittersweet edge. Of course, we made love to each other, of course we still found each other's body sexy, despite the years, the new sags and droops. We were each other's favorite person, and didn't need anything more. But biology has its way.

The suppository Andy uses to achieve an erection (a feat of modern medicine and perseverance) had gone in incorrectly. "Oops, I'm bleeding," he said. I looked down to see blood dripping from his penis, down onto his hand.

The next moment is a blur. I went into action, getting towels, turning on the water in the sink. These were moves I'd perfected since childhood to handle scraped knees and scratched elbows. Now there was another purpose, one that I didn't want to think about. My husband was bleeding and that night's love-making had all but come to an end.

If I close my eyes, I can feel it. The urgency, the fear. I imagine the coppery taste of blood on my tongue.

I try to suppress this image as I lay there on the daybed, scrolling through pictures of men. Men showing off impressive cocks, bulging pecs and biceps. "See," they say. "I'm whole and complete! You can have me!"

Some men "woof" – showing their interest by just pressing a bear paw (why bears 'woof' still confounds me). To a few of these men I 'woof' back, others I ignore. Soon Bryan— who lives 5 miles away— is hitting me up. "How ya doing?" "You look hot" "busy day" "still horny." Mindless missives typed with cramped fingers, all in hopes of achieving something more.

"What you doing?" "Wanna come over?" "Gee I'd love to it's too late," "What have you got in mind?" I seem to hook a live one, a furry stud I'd flirted with before online.

But it's not me he's really interested in. I am hidden, in the shadows.

Our Scruff profile picture is Andy, the hot hairy stud. Dig a little deeper and you'll find me, peering over his shoulder in one shot, smiling coyly in another. But Andy is the bait. Andy has always been the bait. I am the concoctor of dreams, of fables, of promises. While Andy's photo grabs their attention, I create the story, the context. I am the communicator.

I don't intend to have anyone come over actually, although I ask them to meet me, drop their pants. I promise I'll do anything for them, offer them all kinds of a good time.

One by one they peel off, it's too late, work tomorrow. None of them have any more intention of stepping out than I do. They are horny, bored, need one last push to get them off, the promise of a flirtation, of random sex, enough of a nudge to help them find that sweet after glow and drift off to sleep.

Maybe this is what I am looking for too. I've never cheated on Andy, never wanted to. I know we are in this together, that we will weather this current situation as we slip from the young men we once were, to the seniors we are rapidly becoming.

But I don't want to be a senior— not yet. I've never had a wild period like Andy, like most of my friends. No random hookups, no anonymous sex. My freshman college boyfriend lasted 12 years. And only a handful of dates stood between me and Andy and our 28 years together.

I am not the one who is hampered. I am not the one who has challenges. I still feel young, still feel the yearning need to get off. While Andy's biology is collapsing around him, mine is rising up in anger, trying to claim its rightful place, forcing my libido to reach out.

I make no plans.

But inside I am cheating. Inside I am doing everything imaginable to wipe away the image of blood oozing, of body parts betraying us. I am trying to imagine someone whole, intact, someone to tell me I am just fine, I am still as sexy and alive and healthy as I ever was.

I know that man is just one room away, his snores now like burbling oatmeal on the stove. I cannot bring myself to do what my libido is begging for, what my ego desperately wants. Since the cancer, since the treatments, Andy's therapy has become part of me. With each drop in his libido, I lose just that much more of myself and my dreams.

I shut down Scruff for the night, closing out any of the lingering conversations of "hey" and "what's up?" I creep back to the bedroom, scratch our kitty, kiss Andy on the forehead, and crawl back into bed. In his sleep he reaches out, as if I'd always been there, as if I'd just rolled away and he is swimming back to me in this sea of sheets. He wraps me in his arms.

I hope to make it through another night. Just one more. I know what is inside me cannot be shut down. It is an ember, hoping to burst into flame, and I am fearful of the blaze.

I lie awake as the night drifts on, Andy's arms tightly wound around my shoulders. I wonder about Graybeard, and CTMan-4Man, and Bryan, and all the others, just out there, just out of reach. Promises in the dark. I snuggle closer to Andy. He is right there. Right next to me. But in so many ways he is unreachable.

Or maybe it's just me.

We Can't Save Each Other Again
by Becca Beberaggi

When I was 14 years old I fell in love with Aidan. He was nerdy, confused, obsessed with videogames and *I'ming*. Aim. Aol. com's infamous chatting service. A place where all 14-year olds at the time would go for mediocre confused late-night conversations. All seeking the same thing. Connection.

Aidan and I met while attending the same music school on the Upper West in Manhattan. We had both been assigned to perform in a new works recital during the summer of 2006. A recital consisting of 7 to 9 pieces of "new" music commenting on the Iraq War. Boring at the time for us since all we really wanted to do was talk about our favorite comedians and what we would do when we finally got out of our screaming homes. A home where Parents were children and children were Parents.

We didn't speak when we both played in that politically driven music recital. We just looked. Look at each other from across the room. Looked and then pretended to be really interested in what was behind the other person's head. I wasn't good with words. But that was all about to change because that was the summer that I had finally convinced my Mother to let me make a Myspace page. It took many hours of assuring her I wouldn't get cyber abducted and that I only had two friends I was interested in talking to. One of them being my older sister, who I shared a bed with, and the other my Aunt who lived in Florida. I had been homeschooled all through my teen years, so I grasped for any opportunity for normalcy outside of my suffocating home.

Once my Mother finally agreed, I immediately created the page. I uploaded a profile picture, I got a crazy layout from Pimpmylayout.com, and then I racked my brain. Who did I have to add? When I thought about it most of my interactions with kids my age were from the music school and a lot of them had more interesting lives than mine. For them those short lived interactions we shared were a speck of dust in their very busy schedules. For me it was the highlight of my week. Would they add me to their top 8?

I knew Aidan's name purely because of the program from the recital. When I looked him up on Myspace.com, my heart raced. His profile picture was of him making an obscene face with a quote that read, "Your dress is pink are your nipples the same color?" I think it was a song lyric. I sent him a friend request immediately. The next morning I checked my Myspace account and not only had he accepted by request, he had written to me "Is that you Becky?"

We quickly exchanged screen names and began a virtual relationship over AIM. It was forbidden. My Parents didn't understand the concept of having friends and his didn't really care. After a week of consistently I'Ming, he called me on my flip phone and asked me to get pizza with him. My stomach gave birth to a million butterflies. I smiled. *Yes, the answer was yes!* Then I suddenly heard myself say "No." He paused before saying "Oh, I have to go now. Um, you just rejected me." The truth is, I didn't want to say no, but I knew my Parents would never allow it. I even asked my Mother as a joke if she would let me go, and without taking a breath she said, "No, you don't do things like that." My heart was broken.

"I really like you," he told me in a text later that night. "I like you too," I replied.

The rest of the summer we chatted every day. We learned each other's online schedules. I would normally write in the evening after dinner when he would play online video games, and just like clockwork the little bubble would appear on the upper right hand corner of my screen saying, "Hey."

When summer came to an end and it was time to start music classes again, we made a date to see each other. The plan was I would leave my violin lesson early and he would arrive early for his piano lesson, and we would take a quick 20-minute stroll in Riverside Park before my Dad picked me up. It was exciting and dangerous, but we had to be careful. If my Dad found out, it would be bad. He was a drug addict and loved to find any excuse to be abusive. Aidan assured me it would be okay. It felt like he wanted to save me. I was okay with that.

But the day we met up for that 20-minute walk in the park, something had changed. Even though I was wearing my favorite floral shirt and had shaved my legs, the excitement was gone. Aidan was walking 5 steps ahead of me avoiding eye contact. The stroll ended in 10 minutes.

That night when my Dad dropped me off at home, I checked my phone in the bathroom. There was an unread text from Aidan that said, "I don't know how to say this, but I don't like you anymore." I tried to convince him otherwise, but he didn't want to talk to me anymore. Then as suddenly as it had started, our friendship was over.

10 years later, I still think about Aidan from time to time, which is crazy because I'm in a healthy loving relationship of almost 3 years. Sometimes I even find myself wondering, what would it have been like if we had ended up together? So, a few months ago, I looked Aidan up on Facebook. I found him almost immediately. I held my breath, I laughed and then sent him a friend request. He was online at the same time and accepted within a few minutes. I once again gave birth to a million butterflies. Did he remember me? A few more minutes passed and I received a message alert reading, "Hey, I'm sorry about all that, I was going through a lot." I paused before answering, "Lol, what do you mean?"

After we got over the cordial "how are you's," Aidan confessed to me that he had actually had feelings for me when we were 14 but didn't know what to do with them. I would be lying if I said it didn't feel good to read that. I now knew I wasn't crazy. I became a 14-year old girl again. I blushed. I played sappy love songs. I danced around in my underwear. I role played our in-person conversations.

Over the course of a month or so, we continued to chat. I told him about my current relationship and how happy I was. I told him about the years of abuse I had endured at the hands and words of my father. I told him about my sexual assault. He said his heart broke for me. Then it was his turn, I asked him about his life.

"It's crazy how hard it is to grow up," he said. And then he told me he was in recovery. "Recovery?" I asked. "Yeah," he said.

He was currently participating in a 12 step program. ACA or Adult Child Of Alcoholics. "You might like it," he told me. "Sometimes I don't even need to share, listening helps, too."

He was right, I did like it and started attending meetings the following week. When a child grows up in a substance abuse or dysfunctional household, they grow to need certain things. Drama and chaos. You can become submissive and a people pleaser or you can become the abuser. It's a disease. While going to the meetings, I felt closer to Aidan and my inner child. I felt the bond that we had when we were 14, and I began to grow feelings for him again. So I asked him if he wanted to get a cup of coffee.

We texted and made tentative plans for a Sunday cup of coffee. He asked me if I had any favorite coffee places and when I confessed that I didn't, he said he'd find a nice spot. But when I woke up that Sunday morning, I received a text from him that said, "Hey, I think I'm going to have to get a rain check. I'm pretty tired today."

I felt angry. My stomach hurt and I cried. I omitted to share these emotions with my partner whom I live with because I felt shame. What did I expect to get out of my friendship with Aidan, what did I even want? The following week, I texted him and I asked him why he had canceled. He told me he was tired. Then a day later, I received a text saying, "I feel like you want something from me that I can't give you."

As I have continued to attend ACA meetings, I realized that I didn't want Aidan, I needed him. I wanted to rekindle that familiar feeling of loss and tragedy I felt my entire childhood, because it is much harder to be a survivor that is happy than a survivor that is sad. I wanted him to depend on me the way I depended on him all those years ago. Sadly he was right, I did want something from him. I wanted 14-year-old Becky and 14-year old Aidan to save each other.

My Dungeon Love Affair

by Stephanie Parent

I fell in love with Adam a few months after I began working as a submissive at a dungeon, and in the end, the two relationships were one and the same. My first great love: masochism, submission, pain. I held my wrists out willingly for the ropes that would bind them, and by the time I learned that pain can transform, surprise, betray like any other lover, I feared the knots were tied too tight to ever unravel.

On the surface, practicality and desperation brought me to the dungeon. I'd just turned thirty and had lost my job a few months earlier, and if I wanted to choose what I imagined to be some dark, alluring sexual underworld over a nine-to-five, this seemed like my last opportunity. Really, though, I was determined to finally fill a need I'd known since my earliest memories, when in elementary school, I'd fantasized about being kept in a cage in a harem; a yearning I'd fed as a teenager and twenty-something on Story of O and Belle de Jour. Oh, how I longed to feel the sting of the whip, like Severine in Luis Bunuel's film; but like Severine, I wanted someone to see that desire and force me to submit to it, without my having to ask. Severine looked for abuse in a whorehouse, while I turned to a women-run dungeon in Los Angeles, hidden inside a charming cottage on a major boulevard, where four days a week from 11 a.m. to 5:30 p.m., I allowed men to tie me up, spank me, whip me, humiliate me, for a hundred dollars an hour plus tips.

My first months at the dungeon, I fell half in love with every other man I sessioned with, at least the truly dominant ones. It was a relief to lie on a spanking bench, wearing only a G-string, and absorb the impact of hands and canes and floggers I'd been hungering for my entire life. It hardly mattered who was delivering the punishment—if I wasn't blindfolded, I had my face pressed into the leather bench, allowing myself to slip into a darker world where pain was pleasure, where my ability to take a heavy beating became a source of pride, even of identity. But I wanted to travel further into that world, to do what I couldn't at the dungeon, where sex wasn't allowed—and that was how I found Adam.

It started with another submissive girl I'd met online—someone whose name I can't recall, five years later—because she was curious about working in a dungeon. "There's this guy," she said. "He's not the handsomest, but he keeps himself in great shape, and he's very dominant. I told him where you work, and he thinks you'd be fun to play with." Almost as if fate had arranged it, Adam's apartment was only a few blocks from the dungeon, and a week and a few flirty texts after the girl's comment, I found myself heading straight from work to a very adult "playdate"—and yes, in BDSM, we really do call it "play."

When I walked into Adam's apartment, a very large, big-breasted girl wearing only a collar waited on all fours at his feet. I learned later that Adam had a thing for heavier girls, and I, with my love for yoga and history of anorexia, was an exception to his type. Adam also had a thing for threesomes and foursomes, and yes, with both the collared girl and the girl I'd met online there, we made four. I felt so out of my element that I considered bolting, but I didn't. I did exactly what Adam told me to: I stroked the other girl's hair, I watched him spank her, I let him hit me with a leather strap that left speckled bruises down my thighs. I allowed all three of them to pin me down on the bed, with my red lace bra still on—one of the girls liked it—as Adam and I had sex for the first time. And then I Ubered home, and if someone had asked me whether I'd had a good time, I wouldn't have known how to answer.

Two weeks later, Adam asked me to come over again. As I walked from the dungeon, bathed in California sunshine, even once I'd entered his building and risen three flights in the elevator, I was on the verge of turning around and heading to the bus stop. But I didn't. I opened the door to his apartment, and this time, it was just him. As Adam remembered it later, my eyes kept darting around like I expected another girl to pop out of the closet. He talked about nothing and I sat, quiet and nervous, and then he told me to go turn on the lamp, one of those tall, thin ones that hung over the edge of the sofa. I stood under that lamp, looking for the switch, and he came up behind me and bent me over the sofa, and I was gone. I'd never been possessed so completely, never had anyone read my desires so clearly. It was love at second sight.

Those first months with Adam, those first months at the dungeon, bleed together now in my mind. I don't remember who was the first to use a long, slender cane that left welts across my backside, or to hogtie and gag me so I felt completely at his mercy. But with Adam there was the sex, and after the sex, he would cradle me close for what felt like hours, and so he became the antidote to every pain I experienced, not only the ones he inflicted. And pain, I had discovered, was a miraculous lover: the endorphins released with every stroke of the whip brought on a euphoria like no other, and then, having endured that physical trial, I felt deserving of care and comfort afterwards. As a child who'd experienced the death of a younger sibling, I had always lived with guilt; since I was the one to survive, I needed to prove my right to exist. Physical pain gave me a way to feel punished for my perceived transgressions, to convince myself I had suffered enough, and then, for the first time, to truly accept kindness.

Kindness and comfort turned to more, and over the next three years, Adam and I developed a relationship that went far beyond the physical. On our first Christmas together, he gave me a necklace with a delicate silver key and told me he loved me.

We shared a few magical vacations, including one trip to San Diego that combined a wholesome visit to the zoo, a romantic oceanside dinner, and a threesome in which I experienced double penetration for the first time. I felt safe with Adam, this man who positioned me naked in front of the floor-to-ceiling window of our San Diego hotel room, exposed for all the world to see; and for a time, I believed we'd be together forever.

But Adam liked to use blindfolds even more than the customers at the dungeon, and I found that to make our relationship function, I had to keep that blindfold on more and more of the time. Like any good submissive, I kept my eyes closed when I was told to, refusing to see the escalating signs: when I couldn't come over one night because of work, Adam sent a barrage of angry text messages that lasted over a week; the girls we found for threesomes rarely made repeat visits, because they would invariably inflict some slight to Adam's rather large ego. While I enjoyed humiliation, Adam's brand of it sometimes crossed the line into outright cruelty, as when, while we were having sex, he described in detail sleeping with another girl just a few days earlier. The closer Adam and I became, the more his demand for total control grew, until he wanted to dictate my work schedule in addition to my sexual activities.

While I did my best to keep my blindfold on around Adam, at the dungeon, it was already slipping off. The deeper I fell in love with Adam, the less I wanted to submit to other men; and then, I made the mistake of actually looking at the clients who'd been spanking me and tying me up for over a year. I was dismayed to realize that many of them were ugly, not just physically—though there was plenty of that too, old, overweight men who'd never taken care of themselves—but emotionally, their eyes full of greed with nothing else behind it. For many of these men, I was nothing but an object to be used, and I finally saw myself as worthy of something more. But I kept working at the dungeon—I'd come to rely on the money and the companionship of the other women there, and most of all, I was afraid to abandon something that had once brought me so much meaning.

To Adam, on the other hand, I was always more than an object. Adam had a sweet, protective side that came out in the stuffed animals he surprised me with, the way he cared for my dog like she was his own, the fact that he loved spooning even more than sex. I wanted desperately for Adam's better nature to win out over his angry streak, so I stayed with him much longer than either of us deserved. But by the third year we were together, my relationship to physical pain, the BDSM play that had drawn us together from the beginning, was changing. Not just in the dungeon but with Adam, too, my desire for physical suffering was turning to dread.

The night Adam and I broke up, we had a stupid argument. I wanted to download a yoga tutorial on his laptop while he drove his friend home; he, controlling as ever, didn't want me touching his computer. He left with his friend and texted an order to wait for him on his bed, naked, on all fours. I got in position, but as the minutes ticked by, the tears pooled in my eyes till I could barely keep them inside. When he entered the room and smacked my bottom, there was no euphoria, no release, no deep connection with the dominant delivering my punishment. It just hurt, and when Adam growled out, "This isn't satisfying anymore," his voice cold and disappointed, he spoke for both of us. My love affair with pain was over, and though it broke my heart, my relationship with Adam was as well.

I kept working in the dungeon, grateful for my coworkers' support after the breakup, but submission no longer seemed like the solution it once had been. If I wanted to stay at the dungeon, I needed to begin a new relationship. It was time to start learning to dominate others, rather than submit.

But that's another story.

Six Years In A Sexless Relationship Meant I Had To Learn How To Orgasm All Over Again

by Hattie Gladwell

After being in an unhealthy, sexless relationship for six years, my ability to orgasm disappeared. This was a world away from when I first met my ex.

Meeting on Twitter in 2013, I was eighteen and excited when this gorgeous, funny guy had followed me back. He was twenty and seemed popular with women — so I always felt lucky when he replied to a random tweet or photo of mine.

On a confident whim, after a few weeks of infrequently tweeting one another, I sent him a message telling him how attractive he was. What I didn't know then was that this exchange would turn into my first long-term relationship — and sadly one that I lost myself in. Though I had insecurities like any young woman, I was slim and beautiful. I was confident in my looks, and never had any trouble with men. He told me that I was different than the other girls he had dated (cliché, I know). I was a music student and nothing like the other women he was previously interested in; I think he found me intriguing.

After weeks of messaging and phone calls, we had our first date. He lived 20 minutes away but I didn't drive, so he welcomed me with open arms at the train station. I remember feeling nervous but reassured when he held my hand. Our date was like something from The Notebook — we walked through the woods and even took a boat out on the lake. Still to this day, it is the best date I have ever experienced. We didn't have sex the first time I visited his house, but it was clear we both wanted to. The tension as we laid on the bed together cuddling was something that was hard to ignore.

Our first kiss was passionate, me on top of him as he ran his hands over my (fully clothed) body. I remember he mentioned he was surprised by my sexual confidence, as he had seen me as a woman who was more reserved.

That first, lustfully intense kiss soon turned into an official relationship, and a year of sex so mind-blowing to fully remember. Every day together was spent unable to keep our hands off of each other. We would have sex constantly, everywhere. In the bed, on the floor, up against the door. Outdoors in parks or in public toilets. Upstairs at a party, we even did it on top of a washing machine while it was running, while his mom was in the next room.

Sex with him really allowed me to experience what it was like to be wanted, and how appreciated my body could be. I was so sensitive to his touch. I could orgasm multiple times during each sexual encounter. Even just sitting on top of him in my jeans with his legs in between my thighs was enough to get me off.

Hearing from female friends about how they struggled to orgasm with their partners or hookups made me feel proud of my clearly exceptional sex life and my body's ability to respond to pleasure. But orgasms became a distant memory just a year later, when my relationship — and my sex life — started to crumble.

There are many reasons our relationship had changed; we'd moved in together, I got chronically sick, and my ex was struggling with financial issues due to changing and losing jobs. Instead of coming together as a team to get through it all, we drifted apart. And as a result, our sex life suffered.

It started with rejection. Laying in bed together one night, ready to go to sleep, I remember initiating sex with my ex. We were kissing when I reached out to touch him, and he pushed my hand away and said he didn't want to have sex. I shrugged it off and turned around and pretended to go to sleep. I was confused. I lay there feeling vulnerable and embarrassed. He'd never rejected me before. I hoped it was a one-off. But it wasn't.

As time went on, any attempts to initiate intimacy were rejected, and he had stopped initiating anything, too. Eventually I became scared to initiate anything because I couldn't face the rejection. My confidence was rapidly decreasing and I felt unattractive and unwanted. Instead of naturally initiating, I started simply suggesting sex. I cringe inside looking back at how I would suggest that we could possibly have sex on the weekend. It never happened.

It wasn't just sex that was missing, there wasn't any intimacy. Evenings spent under the covers turned to evenings spent in separate rooms. We no longer spent time cuddled up in front of a movie. We no longer went on dates. Any kisses were pecks that felt unnatural. It wasn't a relationship any more. In fact, it felt more as though we were roommates. We would do things separately. I would see friends and go out for evening drinks while he would stay home gaming all night. If he did go out it was without me. I even went on holiday abroad a couple of times without him because he didn't want to come with me.

Despite feeling lonely and rejected, I tried so hard to make things better. I wanted it to work. I wanted things to go back to how they were. I longed for things to start over again, wishing we could just go back to when we first met. It got to the point where I didn't even actually want sex any more, but I didn't want to admit that the relationship had long been over.

I sat down and talked to him about things a couple of times, and even tried ending the relationship because I was unhappy — and knew he was too, but he would beg me to stay and tell me that he did still want me, he had just got "lazy."

It was hard to comprehend, because though he told me he was still attracted to me, he didn't show it. I continued to stay in the relationship, and in the process I completely lost myself. I stopped making an effort with my appearance and I resorted to emotional eating and gained a lot of weight.

I was a completely different person than when we'd first met and when he had finally left me six years later — for another woman. I wasn't exactly sure how to feel. I was devastated, but also relieved. I was devastated because a six-year relationship that I hadn't had the courage to leave was finally ending. I was hurt that he had met another woman and that he had lied and cheated. I was angry that I had spent so many years feeling bad about myself, completely losing myself along the way. But I was also relieved because it was finally over. I felt like I had been released early from what felt like a never ending contract.

But I was also scared. As I continued to lose my confidence, I had stayed in the relationship out of fear of being alone and never being loved again. I convinced myself that this was as good as it could get. That it was better than nothing. I'd faced so much rejection that the concept of a happy, healthy relationship seemed alien to me. When we finally did split up, all of these fears came to the forefront. However, as it turned out dating wasn't a problem. But my body's reaction to pleasure was.

Just a few weeks later, in an "I'm single, I can do what I want now!' mindset," I joined some dating apps. It was thrilling to flirt with men again and to be paid attention to. To talk sexually with people I was attracted to. To have attention for the first time in a long time. Soon after joining, I met up with someone I briefly knew, and we had sex. It wasn't a good experience, and not one I particularly enjoyed. If anything, it was a revelation: That the unhappy relationship was finally and officially over, now that I had slept with someone else. But one thing I noticed was that I didn't orgasm. This had never been an issue before. As mentioned previously I had always been hyper-sensitive and could usually get off in any position, even fully clothed. I put it down to just being a response to a meaningless hook-up. Maybe I could only come with guys I actually had feelings for. But that wasn't the case.

Three months after the breakup, I met someone who I actually liked, who liked me back. Things quickly progressed after talking over WhatsApp for a few weeks and we met up. A night of wine and bad movies turned into a passionate night of sex. It was incredible to be touched by someone I wanted to touch me. It was amazing to have someone initiate sex with me. It was the best feeling to not be rejected. And the sex was great. But... I still couldn't orgasm. And this went on, and on... and on.

We were having sex multiple times a night for months as casually dating turned into a relationship. I enjoyed the sex, but I just couldn't get off. It was frustrating but also concerning for me because I felt like something was wrong with my body. I worried that I would never be able to orgasm again. That a long, sexless relationship had made my body sexually unresponsive. I also felt guilty that I couldn't get off, like I was disappointing my partner. I worried that he thought he was disappointing me, even though he wasn't.

As we continued to have sex, it's like my brain wouldn't allow me to reach orgasm. I would try my best, but because I was trying so hard the pressure put a mental block on me. I decided to take things upon myself instead when we weren't together. I had never really taken the time to explore my body to find out exactly what made me tick, because I had always relied on someone else to do it. On the nights I was alone, I would spend time under the covers exploring my body to find out what I did and didn't like. I had masturbated before, of course, but it was always with the use of sex toys or while watching porn. I wanted to be able to orgasm from natural touch again.

After several weeks of working to achieve an orgasm by myself with no additional "help", I finally took my new knowledge into the bedroom. I had an open discussion with my partner about what was going on, and the way not being able to orgasm had made me feel. I also explained that it was a me problem, and not

81

a him problem. I somehow gained the courage to tell him that I had been spending time figuring out what got me off, and that I wanted to show him what I liked so that we were both getting the most out of our sex life.

It took a bit of time, admittedly. I had to break down the walls of that mental block and the feeling of pressure on forcing an orgasm. Instead, I decided to look at sex in a different way: If I orgasmed, that was great. If I didn't, that was okay too, because there's always next time. What is important is that the sex is — and feels — good. That it is passionate and intimate. Eventually, without that pressure and no longer looking at having an orgasm as the most important part of sex, an orgasm came naturally. And it was a phenomenal moment, not just because the orgasm was epic or because I hadn't had one in so damn long, but also because it felt like I had reclaimed my body. I had lost a part of myself while being in an unhappy relationship for so long, and it felt like that part had come back. It felt like my body was ready for a new start.

Funnily enough, I didn't actually get off from penetrative sex. And it's something that I still can't do. I don't force it, though. Instead, mutual masturbation has entered our sex life in a massive way. And actually, I prefer this. I find it makes sex more intimate and I love sex where foreplay is involved, it makes it more exciting and it's a nice build up to eventually getting off.

Achieving an orgasm isn't entirely what sex should be about. For me, maintaining that sexual connection is what's most important. But let's face it, orgasms are pretty great, and of course, I love having them. Not just because they feel good - but because they remind me of reclaiming my arousal - and the realization that I am worthy of great sex.

Love and Other Accidents

by Blake Turck

When my very new boyfriend and I suffered a serious accident on our first trip together, I said (dripping with blood), "They say relationships based on extreme circumstances never last…. So, we'll have to base it on sex then." Through an anguished look, he responded, "Speed," and I knew I'd met my soul mate.

I'd never been on vacation with a man before, other than my father. I'd had a serious boyfriend through high school and college, a New Yorker who didn't have a license, and we never left Manhattan. Not even for a trip. Years later, here I was being whisked away to Cancun, after just one month of dating. I was thrilled; usually I could barely get guys to commit to a fifth date let alone initiate a plane ride.

At the hotel, I marveled at our huge suite with a wraparound balcony and private pool. I was celebrating lots of firsts: My first romantic vacation ever but also our first time spending more than 48 hours together. Like any new relationship, finding its groove, the mystery of how it would develop was exciting. At one point while trying to use the hot tub, the showerhead broke, spraying water all over the bed and causing a medley of curse words from my guy's lips. When I giggled, he snapped back "Don't!" I immediately worried. Had I made a mistake? Was this seemingly rage-filled guy going to kill me in my sleep? Or was it just a tempered moment I'd become prematurely given access to instead.

A weekend trip with someone new can make you privy to details you wouldn't have at home. I started observing his mannerisms like a detective. As Jerry Seinfeld's show taught me, bad weather could relegate you both indoors which would be the kiss of relationship death. I didn't have much time to worry or detect because before our trip even started, our chemistry came crashing together in a way I never expected.

I wanted to make a good impression that first night. This meant nervously inhaling copious amounts of all-inclusive cocktails. As drinks and conversation flowed, we soon realized comfort was an unexpected, but unanimous emotion. Our mutual adoration quickly led us back to our room.

Drunk, and intending to passionately move ourselves from balcony to bed, we'd mistaken the glass door for open. Except it was actually closed. We fell through, shattering it completely. Shards of glass landed everywhere. Our marked footprints left a trail from the scene of the crime. To make matters worse, we were also both completely naked.

I was a thirty-one-year-old native New Yorker who teetered between cynicism and spiritualism, always relying on an arsenal of quips and witty banter to thrive. For once, I was totally speechless. Confused and dizzy, sprawled out on the cold, tiled floor, a pool of blood began to form and so did my embarrassment and humiliation. Glancing over, I saw my boyfriend, still a stranger of sorts, laying in the fetal position almost unconscious.

It looked like it could have been the scene of a "Friday night Dateline" episode where a woman went to a resort and was never seen again. A bright yellow caution tape to surround us at any moment. Except, he was still there, and looked much worse than me with a huge, gaping gash on his hand.

I'd never been good with needles or bleeding. But in those moments something unexplainable took over and all the fears and nerves that would typically reverberate through me somehow dissolved.

In the past I feared I was too guarded. There was only one suitor who never made the "you have walls up" comment to me. Ironically it was the same one who was my partner in literally breaking down an entire door.

Through the turmoil, I managed to call the front desk for help. I remember little about leaving the hotel room that night. Once at the hospital, questions were hurled around that I had no clue how to answer. The most obvious was, "what happened?" I stood motionless, biting my lip and unsure how to answer.

"Is your husband allergic to any medication??" They yelled at me.

"Umm, I don't know. We've only been dating a few months!" Though completely unhinged at events unfolding before me, I still conjured up a momentary daydream that this could be my future husband.

As they removed the bandage I'd made him, the nurse said something in Spanish I didn't understand. Then eventually murmured, "He's lucky to have you." Suddenly, in a fog of adrenaline, alcohol, and medicine, a clean hand reached out to me with a barely audible, "I am." I wasn't sure if the response was a product of delirium, but I held his hand tight. We barely knew each other, and yet in that moment I felt closer to him than anyone in the world.

He was wheeled away and I stayed behind. Perched on a chair with my head stuffed inside my sweater, I had a million questions. Would he be okay? What about his male parts, were they intact? Would we laugh about this years from now, or would it just be a crazy memory to recount to someone else? A vacation could push a relationship down good or bad roads. This one seemed to have torpedoed towards a destiny. Which one, I wasn't quite sure.

Finally he emerged from an undetermined room. "Here, I think this belongs to you," the doctor said, handing him off to me like a bag of groceries. Those four words moved through me, THIS BELONGS TO YOU.

The night had started light, and fun, only promising each other a good time. One of our first times truly just getting to know each other. No till-death-do-we part or any scenario that concluded with me taking ownership of someone.

We headed back to the hotel, travelling along the eerily quiet

Cancun strip. Outside the cab window, it looked like a cryptic scene from *I am Legend*. I'd experienced many spring breaks in this town, but had never seen it like this. Ahead of us the sun was breaking on the empty streets, shining a light into our window.

In the end, we were lucky, miraculously coming out unscathed. I had a few minor scrapes and cuts. He had a strip of ten stitches along his hand, serving as a permanent reminder of the dangers of being young, lustful, and intoxicated.

Eight years later we're an adoring couple celebrating three years of marriage. Some moments have been extraordinary and others cloaked in comfortable bliss. But I'm glad our love story began with pain, panic, and bloodshed.

That night cemented our relationship forever. Though I didn't know how much at the time. From the depths of a Mexican hospital and a tainted hotel room, he saw someone who would protect and nurture him. I saw someone strong, who could also be vulnerable and loving. A combination of emotions I'd never experienced before. Wherever the future takes us, I know we'll always protect and watch out for each other, and any other sliding glass doors along the way.

The Joys of Dating an Older Woman

by Joe Duncan

There I was, watching her get ready to accompany a friend to a nice dinner out, putting her makeup on, a nice merlot-colored sweater with matching shoes, skin-tight jeans, and a fierce glance that was anything but childlike, a glance which shifted back and forth from her reflection in the mirror to mine, as we talked while she prepared for an adult night out. I took a moment in silence and let her speak, a brief break from the quips we'd been cracking back and forth, and sat there observing her in sheer amazement: "She is such a powerful woman," I thought…

For the longest time, I didn't date older women when I was younger. It just didn't end up happening, I always seemed to click with women who were younger than me, being the very young personality that I am. But I was certainly missing out. My current relationship is a massive divergence from my usual modus operandi. Maybe it's because I have my life a bit more together, maybe it's because I've sewn my wild oats and lived a full and exuberant life and it's just time for me to settle down and relax with my other half, maybe all of these things play a role in this new joy I've found in now dating an older woman, but what's undeniable is that it has its perks. She has her stuff together, there's no doubt about that. And, when we talk about enjoying one another's presence for a long time to come, we mean business, not just pretty words to woo one another to bed with. We've learned to see fleeting emotions and momentary passions for what they are and she's cautious about saying the wrong thing, lest she gives others the wrong idea. She's careful with her words and I admire this.

While I don't mean to diss younger women, here, because youth has its perks for both men and women alike, and I understand that age is very relative and by no means a sign of maturity, there are still some traits that are more commonly found in older people which are just a damn treat to be around when it comes to dating, such as:

• When an older woman commits to you, she means it. She's lived enough of her life to have shed her whimsical ways and learned not to make rash commitments (we all learn this, hopefully). There's security in this. Even when dating a younger person goes perfectly right, young people, in my experience, are more likely to jump ship when they see someone better come along. As we age, we become more firm in our convictions and take commitments much more seriously.

• They're stand-up people who will support us when we need it, but they'll also expect us to fulfill our obligations and take care of ourselves. It's not a one-way street. Dating an older woman has shown me that support is a two-way street, whereby we're expected to do our part and when we fail, we'll have someone who has our back. This is maturity.

• The sex is great. Popular culture tells us that women begin to like sex more as they get older, that they "hit their stride" after they reach the age of 30, etc., but nobody ever really explains why. The "why" in my view is that women finally become comfortable with their bodies as they get older — yes, it takes that long — and even if they never become completely comfortable with their own bodies (who is?) they at least become more comfortable with the men they're intimate with as time goes on, in most cases. I feel like a sex-positive culture could help women greatly, in this regard.

• She doesn't mince words when it comes to laying out her points, her ideas, her beliefs, and her desires. She tells me straight up like it is, what she wants, and what her expectations are, as do I her, and we're almost always on the same page, because we're clear about where we want to go and what we want to do, as well as what we won't tolerate. I respect that.

- Just because she's older, doesn't mean she can't be hot. Older women can be quite stunning and literally make a room stop, show-stoppers that they can be, and when they do, it's not so much done in a cutesy, sexy way, but rather, the force of sheer elegance. There's something to be said about a youthful playfulness, but everyone takes maturity much more seriously.

- She's unafraid to put me in my place — but it comes from a place of love. If she thinks I'm making a bad decision or a horrible career choice, she tells me bluntly, rather than keeping quiet about it and watching me waste my time on things that might not pan out. She helps me analyze why she thinks what she thinks and tries to demonstrate her opinions.

- She does all of this because she actually listens. Listening is extremely important and I would notice that when I was younger and dating, the conversations were often very much a game of patient waiting to drop the next line that we felt was going to attract the person to us more. This tends to go away. Even sexual advances become quick, like, "I've got work, I've got business to tend to and pets, are we doing this, or what?"

- All of this provides an atmosphere of open communication. The double-edged sword to this idea is that a lot of people probably aren't ready for open communication, because to have it, our ideas and opinions need to stand on their merits, not on our illusions of control.

- I respect her on the deepest of levels. This is both for her accomplishments and the whole-package of who she is. She's able to function on a lot of levels in society and that's admirable. She's overcome a lot in life and that's moving. It's important that we respect who we're with, but before we do this, we need to make sure we respect ourselves, otherwise, people we would respect just intimidate us.

I also think that our society, being one that grew out of the prudish Victorian society of Anglo-America, developed an excessive admiration for youthful femininity at the expense of many amazing, strong, powerful, assertive, and wonderful women out there. Our cultural roots have tried, at times, to banish older women, relegating them to the duty of being married housewives, incapable of sexuality, while nothing could be further from the truth. For many women, this is the time in their lives that they come most alive. This duality of woman is evidence of Patriarchal views which make women appear solely as a sex object. There's nothing wrong with being a sex object, in my view, it's when someone is only a sex object that there's a problem, and much of our culture has tended to view young, unmarried women as "available" while older women who are "supposed to be married" are seen as "off-limits."

An interesting book which details how these bogus ideas of the supposed "naturalness" of youthful women being more attractive is Sex at Dawn: How We Mate, Why We Stray, and What it Means For Modern Relationships. It challenges the notion that these sexual principles are engrained in our biology, and expounds on the fact that cultures all over have had much more varied sexuality than our relatively prudish culture, which tends to place undue value on feminine youth at the expense of all of the rest of women. Again, this itself is a sign that women are only viewed through a lens of reproductive prowess, something that many men have no problem admitting to…if only those men knew how wrong they were…and how dehumanizing.

For men out there who are looking for something a little more serious, a little more down-to-earth, a little more concrete, I genuinely recommend considering dating an older woman. It's not that young people can't possess these traits, many certainly do, but years bestow upon us wisdom and strength, both of which are very necessary ingredients for a profound relationship. I've found it much more fulfilling than I'd ever thought possible before I actually, you know, gave it a shot.

Ten cuidado:
A Lesson in Colorism for Boricuas
(...or, Why Have I Only Dated
White People?)
by Elena Fernández Collins

"Cuidao por allá, mija," my Puerto Rican history teacher told me on my last day of high school. "Van a pensarte exótica,"

You'll be exotic to them. Be careful.

Them. White people. White men, in particular.

He didn't know all the other secrets I carried within myself — my bisexuality, my draw towards polyamory, the nugget of doubt about the value of my femininity — and without it, he couldn't warn me against the approach of the world to these aspects as indicators of consumability.

I'll be honest, I thought he was full of shit. At eighteen and in the bottom rung of the high school food chain, being "exotic" did not rate on my list of concerns about moving from Puerto Rico, where I had been all my life, to Portland, Oregon. A city which, if you judged the distance from the reactions of all of my peers' parents and teachers instead of a map, was on the other side of the world. All I wanted was to be interesting enough and smart enough for the prestigious private liberal arts college I had gotten into.

At age twenty-six, I didn't know that I would anxiously ask myself for the first time, avoiding my own gaze in the mirror: why have I only ever dated white people?

Over the decade, I would learn that what my history teacher was speaking about was more than just the exotic Latina girlfriend stereotype, and that I would have a lot of unpacking to do. He knew, more than I did, that the fact that I was white-passing, both in body and voice, meant that I would be thought of as a safe sexual venture with palatable exoticism. And he also knew, much more than I did, that the colorism rampant in Latin American communities had likely subconsciously taken hold of me. He already knew that Puerto Rico's colorism, and especially the colorism present in my English-immersion private school, would impact both the way people approached me romantically and sexually, and who I chose to have those relationships with.

Portland, Oregon is one of the whitest major cities in the United States. There's no escaping the fact that over seventy percent of residents identify as non-Latine whites. The college I went to was predominantly (excruciatingly) white as well; I knew the names of pretty much every Latin American person on campus. I attempted to settle with the answer to this question as one of numbers and averages. Due to my education and my surroundings, I am simply more likely to know white people who meet my dating criteria.

Unfortunately, it's been a decade since I moved to Portland, and since then I have graduated college, gone to graduate school in a city mostly composed of Latin American residents, and participated in Latinx queer Pride events and organizations. I am polyamorous, bisexual, and genderfluid, and have been in an excellent relationship for five years with someone who would fully support and encourage me seeing other people as well. I still… have only ever dated white people.

In paralysis over this fact, I have not even attempted to date anyone other than my current partner in the past five years.

Colorism in the Latin American community is horrific and rampant, the ghost leftover from when Spain implemented a racial caste system with Spanish whites at the top followed by a descending, complicated mess of combinations that ends with children of Black and Indigenous parents at the bottom. Light-skinned and white-passing Latin American people not only benefit from white supremacy, but perpetuate it in their communities and in their relationships, an overt bias towards light-skinned folks as viable long-term partners and parents, and an equally overt fetishization of our darker-skinned community members as sexual objects.

I could list off statistics from a slew of studies, starting with the Lewis Mumford Center's 2003 study that showed white Latines earn more money and have the lowest rates of unemployment and poverty[1], or the 2015 study that showed lighter-skinned Latines are more likely to be seen as intelligent by whites.[2] I could point to the racist reactions in 2019 when Miss South Africa won Miss Universe, and Miss Puerto Rico won runner-up, and the way white and light-skinned Puerto Ricans spent actual air time saying Miss South Africa wasn't beautiful.[3]

I could spend many inches of text talking about research into the role of colorism in Latin American communities in the United States and in their home countries. I could, perhaps, pin it all around the refrain I remember hearing on the island as a child: "tenemos que mejorar la raza". We must improve the race.

Lola Méndez, in the essay "My Latino Father Wants Me to Marry a White Man", describes coming home after breaking-up with a Spaniard whose mother was from Honduras. "At the

---

[1] John R. Logan, "How Race Counts for Hispanic Americans," July 14 2003, Lewis Mumford Center, University of Albany: http://mumford.albany.edu/census/BlackLatinoReport/BlackLatinoReport.pdf.

[2] Lance Hannon, "White Colorism," Social Currents 2, no. 1 (2015): https://journals.sagepub.com/doi/10.1177/2329496514558628.

[3] Susanne Ramirez de Arellano, "Puerto Ricans' Miss Universe response shows racism isn't just for white people," NBC News; THINK, December 15, 2019, https://www.nbcnews.com/think/opinion/puerto-ricans-miss-universe-response-shows-racism-isn-t-just-ncna1102061.

airport, after letting out a slew of sentence-long curses in Spanish, he looked me dead in the eye and told me he hoped that I'd now finally marry a white, American man."[4]

Colorism is ingrained into us. It's born from a protective perceived need to assimilate, to avoid the racism embedded in oppressive structures and the micro-aggressions embedded in everyday living. We can't pretend it doesn't exist, even though white Latines are very good at doing so. And we can't pretend it doesn't come back to hurt us anyway, either.

I have met more than one cab or Lyft driver who would, upon finding out that I'm Puerto Rican during small talk, tell me immediately about his feisty Puerto Rican ex-girlfriend who would fight with him all the time.[5] I never expected to end up sharing more than a half-hour ride to an airport with that person, but then I had sex with one.

And another.

And another.

I had a few longer stays with boys who were the very picture of whiteness: blonde hair and blue eyes, rich families, and corn-bred Americana. I had flings with hipster women who were surprised I gave head and with vaguely creepy men passing through town who I barely knew. I craved physical contact and validation of my sexual prowess like I needed my next breath, but rarely stopped to think who I was getting it all from.

My sex got kinkier, which meant my relationships, however brief, became even more explicitly coded with authority as I explored submission and took to it like a bird to the air. I didn't

---

[4] Lola Méndez, "My Latino Father Wants Me to Marry a White Man," The Oprah Magazine, October 14, 2019, https://www.oprahmag.com/life/relationships-love/a29462752/latino-dating-outside-race/.

[5] She is always an ex-girlfriend. If she isn't feisty, she's fiery or "piquante" pronounced like an American who forgot that it was supposed to be a word in Spanish halfway through.

just crave contact, I wanted it to hurt. I didn't just crave validation, I wanted it to be condescending and kind all at once.

It meant that the first time a white man, while he had me pinned to the bed, mocked the pronunciation of my name-- uh-laaaaaayyyy-nuh[6], a disgusting and unnecessary drawled flat vowel in the middle — I was at a loss of what to do. Did I, in the middle of a scene that I had previously been enjoying, ask him to not pronounce my name that way? Was I supposed to call yellow over this? I said nothing.

It meant that the second time a white man, while he was whipping my thighs as I cried, mocked my mother tongue — aw, sheeka BOW-nee-tah — and continued to purposefully fake his way through Spanish. While condescending to me, I tried to yellow out to say, "Hey, actually, that's not hot," without ending up into a spiel about how that's actually xenophobic, at minimum. Speeches about xenophobia lose their oomph if you're handcuffed to bedposts.

"Oh, don't cry, baby, you'll ruin the mood."

Right. The mood.

It meant that the third time a white man, while he was fucking me with my hair in his hands, demanded that I yell and beg in Spanish while he came, my brain short-circuited. What? I said nothing at all because I was too baffled. He came anyway, and expressed his disappointment before coaching me into calling him "sir" in Spanish.

Even in situations where I have negotiated what I want and don't want, I forgot that society's realities live even there, in a space that was supposed to be safe. White people are at the top and

---

[6] My white grandmother had the unfortunate habit of using the American pronunciation for my name. It's really not sexy to think about your grandmother in the middle of a scene.

what they say, goes. If I didn't negotiate specifically to not use my first language as a tool of humiliation, then clearly it was up for grabs as an option. This power differential, these lingering castes created by white supremacy, invades everything; I don't think I realized how much until then.

Why, after these experiences, would I continue to date white people? Masochism doesn't work like *that*, surely?

It led to the inevitable follow-up question: what was *wrong* with me?

Everything.

Everything was wrong with me.

When I had the first dawning moment of realization about the cycle I was trapped in, I determined that I should never date again for my own sake and the sake of others. I had trapped myself in a feedback loop that was fed by my bias, ingrained into me by my culture and my community, and there was no safe way out except to simply not.

Instead, I inhaled every article and book I could come across that could, perhaps, guide me in surgically removing this disease — colorism — that had been festering without me noticing, even while I knew it existed outside of myself. I read accounts of people who have suffered at the hands of racism and colorism in the Latinx community like my own personal doomscroll, until I ended up sobbing in my bed from this pain I was taking into myself, as punishment. Even masturbation took on an edge of horror for me, when I imagined the skin color of my mind's faceless lovers and recoiled from the fantasy and my body as my anxiety ran away with my focus.

In public, I suffered in silence. My relationships teetered around in confusion like dying wind-up dolls, and they didn't even know why. My anxiety and depression worsened, as did my self-esteem, which was already in its own special pit of hell. There didn't seem to be a way out of the Escherian loop I had created, where I wanted to date non-white people but was terrified of doing so in case they all felt like I just wanted to date them because they weren't white and I needed to feel better about myself.

I'm not sure at what point inspiration struck, but I finally made a rational decision: I brought it up in therapy. When I tell white people and white-passing people in my communities now that I understand how twisted and gnarled the journey towards comprehending how you have perpetuated white supremacy is, they sometimes don't believe me. I look and act like I have all of my shit figured out, because that's what the internet provides: a veneer of both solemnity and sagacity.

So, why have I dated only white people?

The answer is as ugly and nebulous as the path to getting into its general vicinity.

One: Our brains, when exposed to the same traumatic experience repeatedly, revert to that situation as safety because it is a known quantity. The xenophobia of white people was a known quantity to me. In a position of power, they would make fun of my name, or the way I love the Spanish language by mocking it or my accent, or get off on the fact that I wasn't quite white enough.

That I was exotic.

And more than that, that my exoticism was consumable and pliable, something that they could eat for their own gain and use to

97

control me and my body. They felt safe doing so, because they were in power in the bedroom and in the societal structures we lived in.

Let me be explicit. I am white-passing. My Latinidad can hide and it means that I don't scare white people by being too Other. For a moment, they will act with me like they do with other white people. But when my Latinidad cannot be obscured, the power dynamics become clear: they sit at the top of this ladder, and they will reach down from above and touch, shape, and use my body and my service to fit their perspective. The world had taught them that this was not only acceptable, but expected. The world had taught me that too.

Two: I did not want to do the work. That's it, really.

I did not want to interrogate myself or my relationships, and the people I was with certainly were not interested in joining me in that activity. It was uncomfortable and painful, doubly so to do it alone and ashamed. God, what an atrocious feeling.

The work is never over. It's a constant process of checking myself, and being careful and considerate, and always learning. It's knowing that I do, actually, deserve to have romantic or sexual relationships with people from my own culture so that I can connect with them in ways I can't with a white partner. It's not about assuaging myself or patting myself on the back for "a job well done." It's about being critical about my choices, but not so negatively critical that I am paralyzed from ever making one again.

That is no way to live. That's not how we dismantle the oppressive systems within ourselves. I have to make the choice, every day, to correct the imbalance engraved into me. Those critiques and those corrections should happen not in isolation either, but in professional spaces like therapy and in constant conversation with the outside world.

It'll keep the dark from closing in too close.

Sometimes, I hear the ghost of my teacher whispering, "Ten cuidado!" whenever I contemplate what it would be like to meet someone new, or even sometimes when I'm with my partner, who does all this work with me. He won't leave me alone, but I've accepted his presence as what it is: a reminder that I need to be kind to myself, and that the world needs me to watch where I step.

Weight and Dates

by Lisa Levy

I spent most of my life at a weight I'd describe as medium. I was embarrassed about bathing suits — especially because I have big breasts — but not totally repulsed by myself. When I was 16, I liked wearing short skirts, even though a friend later said, gesturing toward my chest with her eyes, "No one is ever going to love you for those legs."

Little did I know that my medium status would not last forever. In my early 30s, after gaining a significant amount of weight because of medicating my anxiety and depression (and dealing with the onset of the migraine headaches, which caused me to both vomit and to seriously crave chocolate cake), I was no longer medium. I was Large and felt Larger all the time. I was so miserable about the headaches, which were a foray into intense pain I had never experienced before, I wasn't thinking much about my weight. But it was happening nonetheless: I kept switching meds, I kept gaining weight, and I kept getting debilitating headaches.

I was thin now, and my life was categorically different.

Clothes that no longer fit were put into garbage bags and shoved under my bed. I cried as I popped buttons and broke zippers. I'd fucked up — for a girl like me, being fat was among the worst ways of paying one's parents back for the years of tennis lessons and orthodontia and SAT tutors and a separate phone line. My academic accomplishments — graduating Phi Beta Kappa and Summa Cum Laude from Berkeley, getting a Master's — meant nothing compared to being fat. I had to fix it. After much therapy, I don't think I was doing it to punish my parents as much as myself.

I started walking in Riverside Park every morning, and because of the migraines, I went on a severe elimination diet, which also nixed alcohol. I was on and off meds so quickly it was hard to tell which ones made me gain weight. I told my psychopharmacologist I'd been trying to lose weight and planned to lose more. Somehow, I did it.

I was thin now, and my life was categorically different. I couldn't believe how much better the service was when you were conventionally pretty: it was like an upgrade to first-class in life. I got free eggplant parmesan sandwiches at the pizza parlor on my block. I got the attention of bartenders much faster, and I got more free drinks once I started drinking again. I got helped in the hardware store and had doors opened for me at restaurants. I had never owned a bikini, so my girlfriends took me to a drunken brunch to loosen me up and then to the insanely expensive but chic Malia Mills. I wore strapless dresses for the first time and bought matching bra and underwear sets. I was proud of this body I'd transformed through sweat and sacrifice, this body that continued to torture me with headaches, this body I swore would never get fat again.

I was astonished at how much my self-esteem and my place in the world fluctuated with my weight. When I was large, I assumed my misery was because of my health issues, but it was also deeply connected to how I thought about myself and how others perceived me. When I was thin, I was more confident. Activities that had made me uncomfortable, like clothes shopping with my friends, were no big deal now. The most dramatic reaction was from my mother, who cried tears of joy when she saw me at my new size. I hadn't realized how much she was invested in my weight, even though my childhood was full of pointed glances and the occasional cutting remark when I helped myself to seconds at dinner or raided the snack cabinet she kept stocked with sweet and savory treats after school.

I began dating again during the time I was dieting and after I got thin. Skinny dating was different, more Man Chase Woman than the kind of moony crushes I'd had before. I felt I had done all of this inner work to be as close to the ideal of intellectual femininity I worshipped — I read and wrote about Susan Sontag and Sylvia Plath and Virginia Woolf, who all had their own struggles with food and men. But once I was thin, I became self-conscious in a different way. I didn't want to be one of those semi-good-looking girlfriends of an ugly genius, even a charismatic one like Bob Dylan (an asshole) or John Berryman (a raging alcoholic asshole). But then I didn't feel like I really deserved a Ted Hughes (actually, also an asshole), one of those storied Adonises who could chop wood, think deep thoughts, kiss you till you bled, and write like a dream. And what about me, what look or style could I contribute to the workings of genius? Was it in me at all?

As a thin person I slipped out of comfortable nerd territory into a much more dangerous neighborhood where people really were judged by their appearances. It was like discovering Santa wasn't real to live the reality of a pretty girl; before I often drifted into friend territory, or was one of the dudes, so I knew what guys talked about and how most of them treated women. It shocked me how judgmental guys were, and these were not even the guys who had been born lucky, rich, handsome or charismatic. These were schlubby, smart, neurotic guys too attached to their mothers, or frustrated with their professional lives, or wandering the world in disbelief that no drop-dead gorgeous woman would be more than happy to laugh at their Family Guy jokes and eat Spaghetti-Os with them on their Craigslist couches. I heard guys at parties talking as if we were all still at Junior Prom, speculating on what certain women would and would not do (and what the guys would like to do them as if these women were at their disposal). It was awful, not as awful as when the guys fucked you and didn't call; or maybe just as awful as when they fucked you, called, and didn't really say anything except they were really busy; or when they wouldn't fuck you for some inexplicable reason, leaving you confused and a little angry.

"According to this fancy math, we should be in love already."

When I was between boyfriends, I sometimes went back to one of the first people I dated when I was getting thin. We'd have endless conversations in which he insisted falling in love wasn't possible, it was a construct, it never lasted, etc., while I'd tepidly argue the other side, a cynical yet practical romantic. Even though he seemed totally enamored of me, he had dumped me years before and then wormed his way back into my life against my strict no recycling rule (i.e. no hooking up with exes, ever). He tortured himself and me by setting up an arbitrary choice between his recent ex-girlfriend and me. He oscillated, and I was the asshole who let him until one night I called him and he was with her.

Something snapped. That was it. I was better than him in all kinds of ways — better job, better writing career, better apartment, better friends. And I was thin, which gave me a newfound respect for my body and for myself. I was not playing this game anymore. I deleted all of his texts and emails.

Soon after, I decided to get over him officially using that classic method of meeting someone else. I went on a dating site that used an algorithm to pair people; after some browsing I found this guy who lived in my neighborhood and seemed like a good prospect (e.g. no Ayn Rand, Simpsons quotes, or references to polyamory). We were a 98 percent match. I wrote to him, "According to this fancy math, we should be in love already." Our romance — in contrast to my recent multivalent, multi-year torture — was sweet and fast. He believed in love, and I did too.

I told my ex to lose my number. He persisted, emailing and

texting and even LinkedIn-ing me to see if I was happy, though I don't think my happiness negated the contempt he felt for me. Now I unabashedly believed in love again, because I was in it. I married the 98 percent guy; we got engaged two months after we met, and since then it's like being on the best date of our lives. Love, like the migraines, took me by surprise. Nine years later, I still have headaches, but I also have my husband.

Kink-Adoring Human Being

by Marcus K. Dowling

Getting raped wasn't the worst thing that happened. It's the fact that I was raped while being a closeted kinky person. That was worse. However, some 20 years later, not having the will or ability to embrace and accept my sexualized social self when I was a teenager has impacted me. It led me to the point where I have recently learned by loving how I love kink, to love myself — and to love myself right now? It's phenomenal. We all deserve self-care, self-love, and self-respect. Here's my story of how via accepting when, where, how, and why we enjoy our unique and sexual best selves, we all stand to enjoy the best possible lives.

I was a week to the day away from turning 19 when I was raped. It was 6 AM, and three hours prior, I had sneaked down the hallway of her dormitory at the all-girls' Catholic college she was attending in the woods of Massachusetts and knocked three times. "Bro, if they answer the door in boxer shorts, that means they wanna fuck." That's what my roommate, who had also been looped into attending a formal spring dance at this college earlier in the same evening, said. As he said this, I was pacing with stalking, intense, and nervous footsteps in the sparse, barrack-style bandbox of a room meant for male visitors, situated just behind her dormitory's lobby. Fast forward, and after the third knock, the door opened a crack, and a pale face, not the alluring 5'2" body I was ideally hoping was wearing cotton Fruit of the Looms, poked out from behind the door. "Hey," she breathed, from between Victoria's Secret glossy red lips, her eyes staring up, with stereotypical, slightly sleepy, and doe-eyed wonder from under messy, stringy black bangs. "What's up?" she continued. "Can I come in? I meekly responded."

"Oh. Yeah. I'm asleep, though. Hold on. Let me put on some boxers." Oh wow. Boxers.

Once inside the room, we joked about my lack of desire to immediately jump her bones, which she found "cute." About 15 minutes after that, we made out, and our kissing left me aroused. "God, I'd be such a shitty lay right now. I'm sorry. Maybe later?" "Ummm...do you wanna talk about it some more? I'm a virgin." "Oh, wow. Ah, yeah, sure. That is SO sweet." Not much else was said after that. We fell asleep, but only I woke back up, with a start, an hour later. I was caught in what was oddly enough for just about two hours, a kink-related dilemma.

It wasn't that I didn't want to have this sex I was presented with having. Physically, I did. I felt like my body was more than prepared. However, mentally, everything about the situation was all wrong. I'd discovered my interest in kink and fetish play at the age of 13, and from that point forward, it occupied significant space in how I defined myself, largely to...myself. It started as a random encounter with foot fetishization in an AOL chatroom. It had evolved, via continued internet searching, matching my internet-driven kink interests with watching hours of classic pornography on Showtime, HBO, and Cinemax. Then, reading women's empowerment and liberation novels readily available on my mother's bookshelf like Erica Jong's Fear of Flying, Judy Blume's Wifey, and Jackie Collins' Hollywood Wives took it one step further. What later ensued was a full-blown and kink-driven interest in sex and sexuality. But, by 19, I was just at a place where my burgeoning libido for sex in general and how I had cultivated my sexual interests created my first of many disjointed and painful moments that it took two decades to overcome.

It wasn't the sex's explicitness that made kink wonderful back then and makes it so exciting to me now. Instead, it was the confidence shown by those who engaged in sexual behaviors. Confidence was something I sorely needed at 13. I had such a bad outbreak of chickenpox when I was four that it left me with permanent scarring on my face, back, and legs. As well, I was 125 pounds in the fourth grade and diagnosed with childhood obesity.

Moreover, I wore thick, tortoise-shell glasses that only accentuated my nerdiness. Because I grew up poor, I loved going to a public school where uniform-wearing was enforced because it allowed my mother and me the ability to hide our household poverty. Thus, when I saw a BDSM submissive in a leather thong with a red lacquered big toe in his mouth, I was just blown away by the audacity and then alien-ness of it all and wanted, no needed it in my life, immediately. Living vicariously through these kinky films, images, and words, I garnered quasi self-esteem that I could store in the recesses of my mind while in real-time winning spelling bees and school awards, but when it came to actualizing what was becoming my dominant social, sexual, and opposite sex-relational needs, I was woefully inept.

By 19, I was awful at coping with the awkward and kinky spaces in my life that I couldn't quite muster the desire to discuss in public. I was saying out of my mouth that I'd hook up with "insert name here hot girl at the cafeteria." Deeper down though, I already knew that it'd be an older woman who looked like Marilyn Chambers who would be dangling a marabou slipper from her toe, who would probably mother me, spank me, milk me, and softly ease the burden of virginity from off my mind and out of my cock. At that exact moment while I was laying in that bed? None of those things were happening. I was scared, very much emotionally alone, and contemplative. Setting course on my future as a sexualized human being — which since childhood was such a meaningful way that I defined my best self — wasn't going to go precisely to ideal form.

But, back to my story…

I eventually passed out and woke up to her performing oral sex on me. I was erect, and in the haze of waking with a start after an hour of sleep, a condom was being placed on my penis while my wrists were being held down against her mattress, and she lowered herself onto me. Thirty seconds later, I had not achieved an orgasm, and the horrified look on my face as I curled into a ball, burrowed my head into her duvet, and cried said everything that I didn't have the wherewithal to compose the words to say.

"You were hard. You wanted it."

"I did. Just not like that."

The next ten years of my life are best described as being lived in a fog of what I felt was underwhelming sexual activities and relationships that, for me, were heavily based on my ability to lie against my truths wildly. Insofar as kink, I found myself intrigued by BDSM and D/s and dipped my toes in and out of those interests. However, it always felt half-hearted because I knew that I was embodying something entirely different from my vanilla life's actual truths. My reality was exposed in dungeons, sessions, and exploring behaviors that appealed to me since my teenage years.

I may have even created an entire freelance writing career and achieved impressive life goals like having had over a million words published in print and online because I was hiding from these truths well into my 30s, too. I learned this after visiting a psychologist for a few months as I neared 40. When contemplating my existential angst regarding my lack of motivation as a freelance professional in the music industry, I was warned of the ills of projection. If unaware, as a psychological term, "projection" refers to a subconscious defense mechanism that allows undesirable feelings and emotions to be "projected" onto someone or something to deny admitting to or dealing with those feelings.

I was living a life that was a non-rope play engaged double bind. On the one hand, I was kinky as hell and lying to myself and the world by presenting as this ultra vanilla person. I either never discussed sex, or in doing so, told lies or attempted to engage in stereotypical straight, cis-gendered male sexual behavior so glorious that it would allow me to shut down conversation at my actual core humanity. On the other hand, I was a rape victim who, in living with and through having my humanity, trust, and self-identity violated, was just floating in a metaphorical sea of anger and self-doubt. However, with a little bit of help from my psychologist, a reawakening of my karmic soul, plus a full reconnection with and total embrace of my kinky self, I have effectively begun the process of healing from my past.

It all started with learning about the concept of projection. I had projected my anger and depression about my perceived sexual failures of the past into working incredibly hard at just about any and everything that would disengage me from having to have any manner of sexual interactions. Releasing that energy has still created a space for me as a rudderless ship of a professional at age 41, making my ability to do very abstract work very well into a significant economic saving grace.

The immediate fear related to the idea that I had solved an issue I'd had for 20 years is what led me to the proactive and energy reclaiming practice of aligning my chakras via tantric meditation. Intriguingly, I was born Roman Catholic. As soon as my mind turned left into kink and body-slammed headlong into the shame of rape, I effectively disengaged my interest in organized Christianity. Yoga, while not a religion, is intrinsically spiritual. When needing to search for a functioning hub in which I could channel my mind, desires, and well-being, tantric yoga has provided salvation. The notion that there were seven chakras, aka "subtle energy centers" that, when aligned, provide spiritual development by finding the ties that can positively bind our unique experiences and memories, was exciting. Couple that with so many of the triggering experiences of my past were finding a resolution via psychoanalysis, and I feel aggressively good about myself.

This level of aggressive peace I feel coursing through my veins has effectively led me back to engaging with the seemingly all-encompassing kink-driven drive of my teenage years. It honestly feels like if I do right by these first, then my chakras will genuinely be in full alignment. I will discover my true best personal and professional self with a positively vibrating, energetic spirit.

Most crucial of late in my development is accepting the idea that kink is not a monolithic thing. What started for me as an interest in toes and soles that became a desire to engage in well defined, safe, sane, and consensual play has advanced much further. Once again, I've been engaging with porn and kink-related material in much the same manner I did when I was 13. Films, books, videos, and now social media, too. Couple this with not having, or more importantly, wanting, to feel any sort of shame or anger about my desires, and I am where I am. There's a more risk-aware and consensual note to my play and interests now. Given my love and understanding of how minds and bodies store and release energy, my desires are far more driven by understanding each person I meet on a situational basis and allowing how we commingle-identify how a scene, session, or relationship ensues.

It was in being unsure of my wants, afraid of my needs, and having my body and spirit woefully misaligned that led me to even being in a situation where I was victimized. This statement is not to denigrate anyone else's rape story. Instead, it is a way to define just how deep into a pit of despair one can fall by not allowing oneself to appreciate the natural purity of their desires and needs for physical and spiritual well-being. I'm a pain slut, pleasure doll, fetishist, and generally kink-adoring human being. Before I define myself as anything else, that is who I am first and best. And that's okay.

The Hoe Phase

by D. Anne Tolentino

A tall, indie white boy with zero emotional intelligence broke my heart. It was the end of my freshman year of college. (Call it the classic liberal arts school experience. I think that should entitle me to financial compensation, but I digress.) So I set out to have a hoe phase. Meaning I was going to have casual partners, a lot of no-strings sex. I had spent the entirety of my first year of college in a relationship while everyone else seemed to be exploring their sexualities. Now, it was my turn. I had never had casual sex before — I'd only slept with people I was in relationships with — but there's a first time for everything.

The first person I slept with after my breakup was the first person I had ever slept with casually. We went on a few sweet dates, but there weren't really any feelings involved. It was just sex, *good* sex. And I didn't want anything more than that. It honestly blew my mind. Sex, love, and monogamy had long been equated to each other in my head. This due to all the ideas of traditional relationships I'd been presented with throughout my life. I'd never been successful at keeping things casual. But here I was, proving to myself that I *could* hit it and quit it. It was the perfect primer for a summer of hoeing out. When the end of the academic year came, I went back to my hometown for the summer, leaving my new fuck buddy behind with no love lost.

That summer came and went like a blur. I was really taking the phrase "the best way to get over someone is to get under someone else" to heart. I wanted to fuck the memory of my ex out of my brain. I wanted to have as many new experiences and meet as many new people as I could. I had my first one night stand almost as soon as I got back home. I matched with a guy on Tinder, he asked me to come over that night, and I said sure. I got there, we had sex. It was quite insignificant, except for the fact that he kept calling me baby in a way that didn't quite feel right. And he fell asleep right after, so I left. I never saw him again. I felt pretty ambivalent about the whole ordeal. Although, the sex was mediocre, it was still fun to go out, meet a new person, and get some head. There would be quite a few nights like this in the coming years.

It's difficult for me to recall most of the details now. There were a couple of regulars and some one-offs. I remember my best friend had a new boyfriend and we went out to parties where they'd hook me up with his hot friends. There were high points, like getting railed under the stars in the back of a guy's pickup truck. And there were low points, like driving 20 minutes to have sex with a guy just to have him come after two pumps of a handjob. Once, a guy I had been seeing gave me the strongest fucking edible I'd ever had. We had really slow sex that felt incredible because my body was very sensitive. But I was still so high the next morning that I threw up five times and love tapped the back of a car on my way home. I have not had an edible since. A year later he would ask me "what ever happened to us?" To which I replied, "What us?"

The hoe phase, as I understood it, was an exercise in sexual liberation and autonomy that allowed me to focus on and explore my pleasure without being beholden to anyone. But what I didn't understand at the time was my hoe phase's role in perpetuating the need for romantic validation and constant companionship. There were times that I felt really insecure because a guy ghosted me, or times when I felt super undesirable because I wasn't getting matches on Tinder. If the goal was to catch as many men as I could, when would I be satisfied? How many dates was enough to make me feel good enough? There weren't enough matches in the world that would make me feel better about myself. I was making myself feel worse by relying on swipes for dopamine. So after an eventful summer, I took a much-needed break.

I went back to school and studied abroad in The Netherlands at an insular campus with a cohort of about 90. Not one to be a messy bitch, I tried not to hook up with anyone in my program because word gets around in small groups. (I made it two-thirds into the program without fucking anyone in my class, huge accomplishment!) I mostly focused my energy on my new friends, traveling, and living in the moment. I actually felt comfortable being alone. It was honestly the happiest I had felt for a long time.

When I returned from abroad, I felt refreshed, confident, and ready to fuck around again. I decided to retool my hookup system. I previously made an effort to emotionally detach myself from the people I had sex with. Now, I wanted to be more intentional with how I was spending my time. I wanted to find a few people who I could see on a regular basis, on rotation, that I really enjoyed hanging out with. In my head, I figured if I saw two or three regular partners at a time, it would help me avoid simping over any one of them. For my own self-preservation, I had to establish clear boundaries between myself and them, so I kept my relationships in the bedroom.

But in the bedroom, I found that I had been missing a particular closeness with my partners. I had been avoiding emotional connection as a way to protect myself, but closing myself off had left me feeling pretty lonely. One day, one of my friends with benefits looked me in the eyes and called me beautiful during our post-sex cuddle and it made me shy.

If you think my standards for men were pretty low, you would be mostly right. The bar was indeed on the floor, but in my defense I wasn't looking for a husband I was looking for a fuck buddy. So yes, *that* comment made me shy because it felt authentic. I was used to physical intimacy by then. I was used to the performance of sex. I was used to being called hot or sexy while someone was inside me. It was all a part of the act. But this was outside of sex. The sex was done. I felt vulnerable and he seemed genuine. I was very emotionally guarded at the time and I'll admit this made me feel some type of way. This wasn't about my talent in bed or my body. It was about me, as a person, and it was a very sweet moment.

The consistency of my partners was comforting, and I felt a genuine warmth toward them beyond our physical relationship. We would talk about our lives, our problems, our desires, and our futures. It was nice to have, and to be, an outsider who cared about the little things — the things that you feel most comfortable saying to a near-stranger.

I think that my partners and I were able to fulfill certain needs for each other during points in our lives when everything was constantly in flux. At this point, I was quite focused on school and my career, and I moved around all the time. The process of coming of age and figuring out our own lives, desires, and trajectories didn't leave a lot of time to adequately focus on a serious significant other. I didn't even want one, nor was I emotionally ready for one; and I knew that despite how much I liked these guys in bed, they weren't the ones I wanted to be with in the long run. But sometimes you need physical and emotional intimacy, even if just for a couple of hours. Touch, during a time of uncertainty, can bring a lot of comfort, so can listening to another person talk about their lives. It takes you out of yourself and your life and brings a moment of perspective.

By the start of 2019, I was fatigued over dating apps and I was growing tired of focusing my energy on relationships I knew weren't going anywhere. I had also been dissatisfied with the amount of mediocre sex I was having. It became very apparent that a lot of the men I saw had coasted on their looks instead of spending the time learning how to please women. I kept meeting men (boys, rather) who would eat me out for five seconds, who couldn't find my clit, or who would just stick it in dry and hope for the best. It just stopped being worth it to me. Good sex is an important part of my romantic relationships, so why was I spending so much time having bad sex?

I had met a handful of partners who I really liked and was sexually compatible with. I started taking note of the qualities I wanted in a long term romantic partner. I felt ready for something a little more serious but hadn't found the right person. I caught feelings for one of my friends with benefits, but it wasn't really mutual (although we kept seeing each other on and off after we ended things romantically, which, as you could imagine, hurt my feelings!).

I took a break from apps entirely. My hoe phase was turning into a lot more emotional and physical work than fun. For a while, my long-term partner was my trusty vibrator that never failed to satisfy me.

I got back on the apps in late 2019, intending to get back on my hoe horse. I met my now-partner on Bumble (which always has better selection, I think) during this time. The previous two years of one night stands and rotating friends with benefits had shown me a lot about what I like in bed and in a person. I really enjoyed the freedom of my hoe phase, but I also wanted more depth and emotion. I found someone who understood this, and we have been in an ethically non-monogamous relationship for over a year now.

My hoe phase was a huge period of growth for me, both internally and interpersonally. It didn't solve all my problems with relationships — those extended way further than sex and romance. But during this time, I stopped relying so heavily on other people for validation. I did things for my own pleasure. I admittedly made some bad decisions. Too many to count, but the biggest no-no was sleeping with my exes when I was lonely and needed familiarity. I hurt some feelings and ghosted people. I met really wonderful people. I discovered that I do, in fact, like girls. And perhaps my biggest revelation was discovering the in-betweens of romance and friendship. There is a whole grey world of connections out there.

I think a lot of people have misconceptions about the hoe phase and it is often seen as trivial. Casual sex and relationships are often disregarded as meaningless, even degrading. But experimenting with different types of people helped me see what's out there and what I really liked and wanted, and those are lessons I carry with me in my relationships today.

Karma Is A Car Crash

by Alexandra Hogan

"Am I dead?" I shouted across the expanse between my fragmented car and his. This was the first sound I had made since the wild guttural scream I let out as the collision reverberated through my body.

"Are you okay?" a man's response crawled across the graveyard of disjointed car parts. All my senses began to creep back languidly. I pressed my palm against each surface of my body. Something warm and wet was in my hands, streaking down my fingertips. There had to be more damage somewhere. Nothing felt broken. How could nothing be broken after a collision so intense? Something must be shattered beneath the layers of adrenaline and my tie-dye t-shirt.

"I think so," my voice came out in uncertain waves. My eyes were darting to each surface of the scene. I could see, but my eyes were not absorbing the information. Then a thought shot into my mind, *is this karma?*

"Don't move, we're coming!" a voice called from a seaside home placed gently on the corner of "How did I get here?" and "Oh, I know!" My Volkswagen Beetle's rounded door had impacted into my leg, glass shattered into my temple, and I was still not confident that nothing was broken. The impact was simply too profound.

"Pick up, pick up," I whispered. I could hardly dial my trembling hands, and the tear-drenched touch screen worked in tandem against me. He wasn't answering. I texted his roommate, missing every few letters or so.

"I'm so sorry," the driver of the other car kept repeating as he paced in the spot my headlight should have been shining.

"It's fine. I'm fine, really," I kept assuring. With a deployed airbag next to me and the inability to evacuate the car on my own I still didn't want to inconvenience anyone. The voice that came from the house belonged to a nurse. She brought out a hard-shelled case filled with medical tools. She checked me out with all the precision of a doctor and the soothing care of a mother. I felt more at ease and cared for amid this mess than I had in months.

"We just called the ambulance. They're going to take you to Yale's hospital."

"No," I insisted, "I don't need to go, I'm fine," nothing some time in his bed couldn't fix, I thought to myself. The ambulance arrived like Kramer from Seinfeld, making a huge deal about its entrance onto the scene. The EMTs gingerly removed me from my car after they wrapped a brace around my neck. I apologized for the mess in my car. They helped walk me over to a bench facing the ocean. One asked me questions while another prepared a stretcher.

"I'm assuming this guy is for you?" he pointed past me. I delicately turned my whole body to see him running towards me, out of breath, his hair wet.

"How do I look?" I asked, attempting to melt away the concern on his face.

"You really did it this time, huh?" he pulled out one of his half-smiles and shook his head, but it did little to hide his apprehension. He placed his hand on my shoulder and kissed the top of my head where my hair parts ways. His touch did what it always did: it made me feel like everything was fine, lovely even. He was there, and so was the beach, and the stars, they were there too. Everyone else could go home now, he was there, and I was okay.

"Let's get her onto the stretcher," I heard someone say.

"No, really, I'm okay. I'll be fine," I argued again.

"We have to take you to the hospital and check for other things, internal bleeding, broken ribs, just to be safe." I looked to him for back-up.

"I'll follow you guys there," he said to the EMTs. "Can I get you anything?" he asked, now addressing me. He asked me this ritually, almost every night we had spent together since the first. Ever attentive to my needs, even after nights when he spent hours fulfilling them, he would still ask, "Could I get you anything?" I never got to thank his mother for that. They hoisted me onto the stretcher and wheeled me up into the vehicle for my maiden voyage in an ambulance. I squeezed my eyes shut to block out the harsh light, which was grating on my concussion weary eyes. I heard his voice, and my eyes shot open. He shot up a sign of the horns, and I sent one back through the glass of the window.

"I'm sorry I'm not wearing a bra. I didn't plan for this," I apologized to the EMT.

"This is almost as exciting as my first time in a limo," I added. I waited on the stretcher in the hospital hallway. My phone had died, but I wasn't worried. I knew he would find me. Eventually, I heard him around the corner, and a smile wriggled its way across my face. He was holding a Gatorade — purple, the only kind I can stomach.

"How are you doing?" he asked. I cried a fresh set of tears for something that ached more than my body. He rubbed my calf and watched me silently. He grew impatient quickly, a characteristic of his I had grown to get a kick out of. He inquired with the front desk about why I hadn't been taken care of yet. He pressed again after another fifteen minutes, and we were finally brought into the hospital proper.

"Do you have someone who can take care of you for the next few days?" the nurse asked.

"Yeah, I'll be taking care of her. She's gonna stay with me. I know what to do."

"I'm gonna take her to the beach tomorrow. That'll make her feel better. But don't worry, I'll make sure her eyes are shielded from the sun. I'll set her up good."

"Okay," she laughed. "I'll be back to let you know when they're ready for your CAT Scan." The last thing I wanted was for my mom to have his number, but I knew by now she was freaking out that she hadn't heard from me since my last call through short, strained breaths. I called again. I told her she didn't need to come. He would take care of me, he insisted. She was already halfway there. We sat and talked for a while. Trivial things and serious matters, crashing into each other and coinciding the way our talks had always flowed. We had been this way ever since we started smoking together on the roof after the neighbor's kids were tucked into bed on sticky summer nights. He reached up for my hair, which had turned into a tangled nest of glass and crusted blood.

"Is this wet from a shower or with blood?"

"Both?" I questioned as I sent my own hand to inspect the situation. My fingers excavated glass that was still buried in my skin, and I began picking them out, hurriedly one by one.

"Wait, you're dripping," he protested at the same moment I began to feel the streams of blood roll down the side of my face.

"Just grab a paper towel or something," I said casually. When he asked the woman at the desk for something to wipe some blood up with, she jumped up, alarmed. We were always too relaxed about everything. What could possibly be wrong in the warm glow of this person's company? The nurse ran over with a kit to remove the glass and clean the site. She asked my name. Then she asked,

"And who do we have here?"

"Boyfriend," he blurted out before I could open my mouth. I stared at him with something like contempt, or was it disbelief.

"I'm her boyfriend," he repeated, avoiding eye contact with me. Although I think she was just asking for his name. As she was finishing up, my mom came in nervous, rushed, and laughing about the neck brace. The three of us sat there for hours.

When they called me in for my scan, I was nervous to leave the two of them alone together — this was only the second time they were meeting. They had both heard so much about the other, both good and bad.

"Let's make this quick. I don't want those two to get to too much talking out there," I teased the technician. As I laid on yet another stretcher straight surface, I played back his "girlfriend" comment from earlier. Is he deranged or just delusional? I figured we were each guilty on both accounts.

"Call to mind a peaceful memory," the scan technician softly said. I transported myself to the ocean in Belmar, riding the waves on his surfboard. My body was tired but still yearning for his. The sun was setting behind him, and I knew when it took its final breath, he would be coming home with me. It suddenly felt ironic this mess happened adjacent to the ocean.

"He's going to help us move stuff out Thursday and Friday. He offered his truck," my mom said when I returned. He smiled and nodded along. They informed me of the specifics. It suddenly all felt so clinical and strange to be planning to move my things before I had wrapped my head around leaving my college town — and leaving him.

"So you're going to drive my stuff to New York and then drive back here? I thought you were surfing in Rhode Island Thursday?"

"Yeah, why not? We'll figure it out. Don't sweat it. Let's just get you out of here. How long did they say for the results?" he had an intuitive way of knowing when the conversation needed shifting.

"They said it could be a couple hours." We all sighed. I went to the bathroom. When I dropped my shorts, several shards of glass fell to the floor. I noticed paper-thin cuts along my hips and butt.

"There was glass in my butt," I informed.

"In it?" he asked.

"Well, not like 'in it' in it, but all up in my pants. Look I, have..."

"Alright, you don't need to show the whole hospital," my mom laughed and stopped my hand from trying to peel up my shorts for evidence. I walked to the car with a slow, deliberate gait. I still didn't feel settled back in my body.

"Are you sure you don't mind taking care of her? You know you don't have to. I can—"

"No, no, I want to. We have plans tomorrow. I'll take good care of her, I promise," he said. My mom gave me a long hard look, that meant a hundred different things at once. He opened the car door and helped me up into the seat.

"Can I get you anything on the way home?" *Home.* I sighed.

"No, thanks. Still pretty nauseous." He drove slower after that. By the time we arrived at his place, I felt simultaneously weak but full of a strange energy. I had to shower to wash out the chemicals they used on the side of my head where the glass had dug itself a grave. He gave me a towel with his name sewn into it beside a choo-choo train. I had used this one before. He laid out his comfy clothes for me. I slid them over my body and crawled into his bed, the mattress of which I was very well acquainted — it knew my every angle. However, this bed hardly ever saw me so clothed. He laid next to me, whispering as my eyes fluttered open and shut. We began to kiss because that's what we knew how to do. He propped my head up on a pillow while holding my neck as we moved toward sex.

"Are you up for it?" he asked, knowing the answer. He knew what would make me feel better. He fucked me softly and sweetly, trying valiantly not to cause any discomfort. He went down on me for what felt like an "I'm sorry you got into a horrifying car accident on your way to see me" amount of time. We fell asleep faces touching the way he liked to and the way I'd surprisingly grown used to. I woke up as the sun leaked in. I watched the light bounce off his buoyant butt as he stepped into his shorts. He kissed me goodbye and told me to rest until he got back.

I stretched my body feeling each individual ache. Beneath the pillow, my hand brushed against a material, unlike his cotton sheets. I retrieved a tiny tank top, his girlfriend's, I assumed. *How could I have been so blind as to not stop?* I thought to myself. I couldn't go back to sleep once he left. I called my mom, my dad, my insurance, and my brother — it was his graduation day. The thought of being in a car for possibly four hours was daunting because the nausea had only gotten worse, and so had the headache. As lovely and peaceful as a sun-drenched day with him, and no automobiles, sounded I couldn't fathom missing my brother's graduation, and so my mom's journey back began. I curled up on his back porch. Facing me were four brightly colored surfboards aqua, meringue, amber, and lime. I couldn't recall which one he had taught me to surf on the summer before. I nodded off in the radiance of those memories. I woke to a hand, speckled with golden hair, resting on my back.

"I couldn't sleep," I said.

"I see that," he responded slyly. I told him my mom was on her way. He told me I had to eat something first. I could tell he was disappointed I was leaving. It couldn't match all the times he'd disappointed me. My mom knocked on the door while I was sitting with my legs draped across his sipping the smoothie he made me.

"Come in! Your daughter has to finish her breakfast." The last bit of frothy berries and bananas slid across my tongue. He pulled me in tight and held my head to his chest. I felt the hair beneath his shirt against my cheek as it rose and fell with his breath, this was my comfort zone, but I knew I had to leave it.

"I'm glad you're okay," he said into the top of my head. My mom asked me if we could drive past where the accident had happened. Maybe the accident happened two summers prior when I met him. Perhaps the accident was when I insisted he shouldn't leave his toothbrush at my place, asserting my definition of the relationship without my knowing. No, the accident had to have been when he laid in my bed and by the glow of my night light told me he just started dating someone. The damage was done, after disobeying a no right on red when we carried on like nothing had changed. I directed my mom to the spot where the collision

125

had happened on Ocean Avenue. Although the real collision happened, the night he and I first had sex on a bare mattress in the summer heat until the sun rose through the attic window, cueing us to peel apart from each other. *How could I be so blind as to not stop?* The glass sparkled on the pavement, evidence that beauty can come after destruction. We went to the shop that had towed my car. The car was totaled, as was our relationship — this had to be the end.

My mom and I were speechless in the presence of my car, deeming it impossible I was okay. There had to be more damage somewhere. Nothing felt broken. How could nothing be broken after a collision so intense? Nothing was broken this time — this was a warning.

I can still feel the scars beneath my hair, thin and uneven. I can still feel the scars of his memory, but they run deeper. Leaving him that morning, I was messy and broken, but he looked at me like he had just met me, red lipstick concealing my smile, and that crystallized our relationship. Messy, broken, dazzling.

Never Fucking A Guy Who Has A Podcast Again

by Danielle Chelosky

His mouth was bleeding, but I was waiting for hours and hours. No no no, he texted me.

*

He lives underground. It's always dark. He lets me smoke his Parliaments. I hear the rattle of the train; I wonder if he heard me outside on his stoop on the phone, drunkenly gushing to my best friend: I really like him.

*

Everyone calls my writing "detached." All of my friends tell me to stop getting so "attached."

*

We stay up until 3 or 4 A.M.; I drink a whole bottle of wine, chainsmoke while we get to know each other on his stoop — though I'll forget everything by the next morning — and we fuck twice until he falls asleep.

His alarm goes off and he says: You know it's 9 A.M., right? I groan and ask what we talked about when I was nearly blackout drunk. Let's see, he says, You told me about Father Flanagan's, you explained to me who Ian Cohen is, you wouldn't accept the fact that I don't like Tigers Jaw...

*

To the listeners out there, we're not douchey enough to be in our 30s and have a podcast — a weekly podcast — where we dive into Hunter S. Thompson... we talk about shit like, how I went to the dentist yesterday... let's see, what else do we talk about...

how I was supposed to get a double suck, but then that didn't end up happening... real shit, important shit.

*

My stock went up, he says, and then looks at me and reminds me: I'm old.

*

He told me that he goes to the cafe on Wilson, and I said no, no, not anymore — like I knew what would happen. He refused; he's been here longer, and they like him there, but they like me, too. We walk there together, and I sit outside ready to work while he finishes his cigarette before his dental surgery. He tells me he doesn't have insurance; I assure him that I can insure him.

I open an email from my professor asking if I want to read at an online school event with six undergraduate students and six graduate students. I don't want to, I whine.

You should do it, he said, flicking his cigarette into the street.

*

You don't need to have bad, forgettable sex so you can immortalize it in writing, my friend tells me.

*

As we walk to his place from the liquor store, two days after his dental surgery, he tells me: If we make out later, it has to be soft and slow. I say: Oh, you're vanilla, huh? He says: Yes, I am. I'm not the type to hit a girl on a first date, he jokes, and I blush, remembering us in his bed the night we met, his hand hot and fast against my face.

*

I have Stockholm Syndrome, I tell my friends because I've fucked three people on Stockholm Street.

*

His birthday is a week before Valentine's Day, but he's no romantic, I find that out very soon. She's not my girl, he says on his podcast, She's, uh, doing the Lord's work for me.

*

You can escape me but you can't escape my writing, I tell the world. He likes it.

*

When I ask him if he has any Halloween plans, he says: I was invited to a party, but I can't imagine going and not being able to smoke a cigarette. He has to wait until Tuesday, when his mouth is fully healed, or something like that. It could cause "dry rot" if he smokes now. That even sounds gross, I say about the two words. It sounds like the name of a hardcore band. Days later, I stumble upon @dryrotsc on Twitter — a "screamo/hardcore" group from South Carolina called Dryrot.

For my Halloween, I stay out until 4 A.M. at a bar, where my friends warn me that he's trouble. You should assume that he's talking to at least three other girls, I'm told, but I shake my head, I ignore it; I'm cynical about everything, but I'm naïve with love and sex.

I smoke a whole pack of Parliaments that night; my friend says, You know you can do coke out of them? Because they're ventilated.

*

He asks: Do you have to drink the whole bottle? I do, and I'm glad I do; the altered state of consciousness prevents me from sincere and vulnerable intimacy with him — it shields me, it protects me, it is the only protection we have in that moment.

I like you, I said and this exchange is the only memory I have before everything else turned into a blackout blur—

He replied, and I know this is what he said, this is the one thing I am sure of: I like you, too. Maybe he meant it; he probably didn't. We were both indulging in our intrinsic destructive natures, but I remembered a Louise Gluck quote a friend read to me: "Beauty dies: that is the source / of creation." From our mess, something could be created. I convinced myself of this.

*

He tells me that I can ash my cigarettes in the plants; it apparently helps them, gives them nutrition. Cigarettes are good for you, I figure.

*

His pinned tweet reads: Staring at a condom like it's a fax machine

*

Why am I far removed in my writing? Why am I detached? Instead of using my writing as an outlet for my emotions, I use people themselves — I give them everything, people who don't deserve it, people who don't want it, and then they become shadows in my essays, shadows outlined by my feelings, empty inside, hollow.

*

He tweets: Everyone wants to be on my podcast but no one wants to listen, 5 likes.

I tweet: never fucking a guy who has a podcast again, 46 likes, 3 replies.

*

I ask my friend: How do I not take it personally? He says: It's like the way your fingers get callused from playing guitar. It takes practice. Don't romanticize everything. Stay far removed. Expect the worst. Fake it till you make it.

*

The only thing that stops me from drinking is the sickness that follows — the accusations from my body, the pain of withdrawal, the shaking, the stomachaches, the alcohol in my breath, the near-death feeling.

Instead, I fill my breath with smoke.

*

Honestly, this dude sounds like he's 32 going on 17, my friend tells me. See the red flags. He asks why I always ignore red flags — and the question itself feels like an accusation, or maybe it's just because I know the answer all too well: I am a masochist, I am begging to be hurt. I am always at the bottom of the power dynamic, submissive and waiting for him to hit me another time, flinching at the sight of his hand, half out of fear and half out of excitement. He is twelve years older; I am inherently naïve and predispositioned to be fucked over.

*

My best friend says: No more guys who are comedians or have podcasts bro

*

Guy 1: ...all of it seemed so gross... I feel like the correct response is to catcall. That's the only one... if a dude did that on camera, at least it's the only one that seemed like it would have any type of dignity... If that's what I look like when I stare at asses, then...

Guy 2: How nice was this ass? Was this kind of like a spectac—
Guy 1: Oh, spectacular.

*

We were in this open thing... but she started catching feelings and I noticed that she started catching like deep feelings. And I got a little scared that she was doing that, so I went and quickbanged someone to go and guard myself from the feelings. But since we're in an open relationship, we had to tell each other when we have sex. So that night before I even had sex with the girl I was like, "I'm thinking about having sex with a girl. If this bothers you, I won't." She's like, "No, it's your life, you do what you want."

So, I had sex with this girl, and then that girl happened to listen to our last episode and texted me and was like, "So, you're fucking me and I listen to your podcast and it turns out you're fucking someone else? What's up with that?" So, Danielle, if you're listening, I haven't texted you back. I'm sorry. I mean you know what I mean. We didn't have a thing going, really.

So, anyway

*

I collect the threats my friends offer me about him: "I'd fuck him up for you," "I'll kill him," "Let's cancel him"

*

On Myrtle and Stockholm, I will come to you and make all of your unfunny jokes unfunnier. I will make your gums bleed harder. I will steal all of your cigarettes and light you on fire.

After the Third Strike, How Do We Stay Together?

by Vonnie Wright

The Start

I've been married for eleven years. I got married at 23 years old. One year after graduating from college, and my commission as a 2nd Lt. in the United States Army. One year after graduating from Armor School and my first job as a platoon leader in Fort Benning, Georgia.

I was a bachelor for only 14 months. Let that sink in.

As I dated my wife throughout college for two years, the speed of marriage did not occur to me then. We couldn't have been more different than each other. I grew up in that spectrum between poor and middle class in the South, Charlotte, North Carolina. Also, From ages 8 to 17, I grew up in a divorced household raised by my mother. I'd see my father every other weekend, and we would soak in as much time as we could together. My parents' relationship was bitter, and I was caught right in the middle. The only thing I wanted to do was leave everything behind, so from a young age, my mind was set on following my father and grandfather's footsteps and joining the Army.

Going up and down in wealth, jammed in the middle of my parents' toxic relationship and being told what I can and can't do, fostered certain personality traits that continue to impact my life, especially my relationship with my wife, to this day. I don't trust anyone! And I would rather suffer in silence before I ask anyone for help. Furthermore, I'm a complete introvert. Yet, as if to balance this all out, I'm extremely passionate, intimate, and caring. Aside from being caring, my wife is the complete opposite.

When I met her in college, there wasn't a soul alive on that campus that didn't know her name. She is from Queens, New York. Loud, and a real extrovert — she will have a three-hour conversation with a complete stranger. She enjoys trying new things, interacting with people, and cannot sit in one place for too long. Her openness, honesty, and self-described "healthy sexual appetite" were all things that I welcomed, especially the sex; in our youth, two to three times a day wasn't far-fetched.

When I met her, I was skeptical why she was talking to a "nobody" like me. Being let down for most of my life and witnessing a lot of sick jokes, I was confused. Without a vast amount of experience in the dating department, not trusting anyone or knowing what I had to offer as a broke college student, she initiated what would be her usual role as the aggressor.

After a conversation of where she told me that she was sick of giving me the hint that she wanted to be my girlfriend, I asked her out. And we haven't looked back in 14 years.

How do ya'll even go together?

How does a quiet, reserved, and private gentlemen coincide with a social butterfly that is anything but shy or vanilla? People are still surprised to this day.

With more sexual experience than I had, my wife respected that I never asked her the quantity or quality of her sex life before me. That was a first for her. Those who she dated before me always asked, always wanted to know. Me not asking was a curious beginning to our relationship. It's not surprising that someone as beautiful, bold, and flirtatious as my wife had had their share of fun; but I never wanted to know about it. The only thing that counted for me was that my wife was attracted to me, to my innocence, my sincerity, and the fact that I wasn't selling her a dream. The Yin and Yang philosophy is true.

Opposites attract, but they also collide when they come together.

One thing has consistently worked for my wife and me: Sacrifice. My wife had goals of working on Wall Street, being independent and living in the middle of the city. She even had an internship where she worked her dream job over the summer. But she gave all of that up and followed me wherever I said we had to go because of the military.

Strike one.

Her love for me lead her to leave behind her own aspirations, the chance to always be around family and friends, and the opportunity to have the kind of social life that she really wanted.. Also, lacking the capacity to work, depending on the location due to the military, still remains a death blow. My wife was clear about maintaining her identity as a person, otherwise the marriage wouldn't work. She was adamant about not being a trophy wife or a stay-at-home mom. This was made abundantly clear when our first child was introduced to the equation after 6 weeks.

To overcome this issue, whenever it's time to move, I circle what I need to do to progress a secure a promotion, and I hand over the list to her. I put the ball in her court to wherever she wants to go. As a country homebody, I can live and work anywhere, but I know that she can't. This has been a point of contention since our marriage began. The loss of her identity and her belief that I don't care about anything but my career has led to her nearly walking out.

If there's one element that makes this marriage work, it's sacrifice on both ends. This is also where the Yin and the Yang principle comes into play. As the cooler head and more rational out of the two of us, I don't mind sacrificing what I want to enable her success. Within a relationship you have to be able to step back and see the full picture. I'm in the exact career that I want. She took a close second. Self-reflection within our relationship has been crucial because with my personality, I would never be able to see things her way, especially if my solution doesn't fit her married but still self-sufficient lifestyle.

Which brings me to my internal issue. Her desire for self-sufficiency and independence is both a turn on and an ass-itching irritant. Most people would say that I should be grateful for a woman who has goals and is career focused. And I am. I love that about my wife.

What I don't like is the perception that I'm not needed or the acknowledgment of self-preservation and the backup plan. There is an unspoken distrust on both sides of the equation that could lead to the mutual self-destruction of both of us. Having a career to fall back on means she will never be stranded if I decide to walk out on her. I can't argue with that wisdom, and I think that is a realistic thing to keep in the back of your mind. *Just don't tell me that.*

Now, to be honest, I think the only reason she is so adamant about working is because she is preparing to eventually walk out on me. This fear is bolstered by all of the threats made within our marriage in the past whenever times got rough. Once you plant that seed, it's hard to forget, and it's even harder for me to get over.

Strike two.

Trust is still an issue for both of us. I don't think either of us *completely* trusts the other. She hates the fact that I am a realist and pessimistic. But life made me that way. *She* made me that way. Her phone is consistently flooded with men detailing what they want to do to her. What does this leave me to think? How do you fix that? Complete and total honest communication? Married couples in the military go through scandals, and spouses leave at the drop of a dime.

I told her she was the only one I wanted. She said the same, and told me that I shouldn't worry about who's talking because that doesn't invoke attention. Still, it's hard to believe when you're deployed, or constantly in training and away from your family. But if you can't trust your spouse, who can you trust?

Forced Distance Relationship

Within the complexities of trust and identity awareness, there is distance forced within our relationship due to me having to answer the nation's call.

I trust my wife, but as I mentioned before, she has a strong need for sex and intimacy. I know she feels like a forgotten spouse, and that she's ready to leave me because of that. So despite the trust that I have, any reasonable man would have the same sort of internal "what if" questions as I do. To make matters worse, she has gotten comfortable and used to me being away. Hell, according to her, I even mess up the rhythm of the house upon my return, as she herself is used to being a "single" parent.

Strike Three.

Normally, or in the best case scenario, in the military one would welcome their spouse knowing the drill. They would be used to being self-sustaining while their soldier is separated from their family, ranging anywhere from 1 month to a year. In this case, that trust that you have with each other is a gift and a curse. I'm proud to know that my wife can take care of herself, the house, work, and still look after both of our kids. The problem is, she's vocal that she's comfortable without me being there, but at the same time she tells me that she doesn't want to get used to me not being around. She's also afraid that with the distance, she doesn't know if I will come back changed, or if I'll be comfortable around her, being that I'm away for so long. She is prone to anxiety to the point where it affects her health. So this is a huge worry.

With these tremendous pressures, and her sexual appetite and need for intimacy, we have created a cesspool of bad thoughts and have had difficult conversations you don't expect to have. Like the possibility of "hall passes" and other partners. It started off as a joke, but then grew into a serious, open-minded discussion in the "what if" game — which is a dangerous game to play. In the end, we both agreed that the answer was a solid "No." But even having this conversation adds confusion to the relationship, and causes both of us to have serious doubts about whether either one of us can leave and trust each other to be alone. When you lack sexual satisfaction and you get used to being alone, what happens next?

The only fix that we've found is living in a state of constant, clear communication and admitting again that we only want to be with each other. Additionally, it helps to make plans for exactly what you want to do when you see each other, beyond a simple vacation with the kids. Personally, we have to get graphic with our promises and sexual desires, and it's imperative that we keep those promises. This keeps the relationship fresh as we promise what we will do together on vacation and within the bedroom, bathroom, hotel balcony, closet, car, etc. Yet, you have to cash in on it or this will not work. Nothing is worse than the anticipation of a freaky desire with the one you love and it doesn't come to fruition. Keep your promises. The build-up and anticipation are so strong, it is some of the strongest moments of intimacy you can have.

For example, my wife is not a fan of skinny men or men that are too muscular. She favors those who are husky but fit. She calls it muscular with a bit of fat and a little belly. Not a big belly but a small one. "I want you fit, but not too fit," she told me. That conversation took years of my life that I will never get back, and her disappointment that I will never have a belly to stimulate her clitoris.

I once deployed to Iraq at 6 feet tall and weighing 172 pounds. In the back of my mind, I knew what turned her on and I needed the increased strength. I promised her that I was going to get up to 200 pounds. She only knew me to be skinny with an extremely high metabolism. Between missions in Iraq, I worked out for close to two hours a day, ate four times a day, and drank four protein shakes a day. Within two months, I was 197 pounds. The key was the anticipation and the promise that I kept. I showed her my progress during video calls, and I promised I was going to wear her out as soon as I got home on leave.

I got home on leave and I went to take a shower. As soon as I stepped out, she was right there and begged me to put it in. I made love to her right on the bathroom sink. It wasn't the best sex I had in my life due to me coming home and not being with a woman in over six months. It was the anticipation of keeping our promise to each other. The fact that she wanted me so bad she didn't even let me dry off. The fact that I surprised her with something she didn't dream could happen.

Keeping your promises and communication during a long-distance relationship works.

Friends First

My wife is my best friend. Period. She knows me and I know her. I know what she's thinking, and she can say exactly what I will say without saying it. I know her like the back of my hand. I can go into a store and pick out her entire wardrobe, and she will wear all of it and it will fit her style. I study her. I pay attention to her. I adore her. That is the key. In return, she does the same for me, she pushes me to be the best that I can be. She tells me the truth in the most direct way possible. Anything from "Your breath stinks" to "Take those skinny jeans off, you look nasty."

139

She accepts the fact that I love well-kept feet (she calls it my foot fetish), and I accept the fact that she likes fat guys. No shame on them, but that's just not in my DNA. My wife and I have learned the art of compromise, even on this simple level. She gets a pedicure routinely to keep her feet on my face, and I promise to never fall below 190 pounds.

Things like that might be funny, but without multiple levels of compromise we will fail as a couple. Without honesty and sacrifice we fail as a couple. This is what makes us the epitome of friends. We can be transparent and even argue with a raised voice or two. Give or take an hour or eight. But like the best of friends that we are, we come back to each other and we have a discussion and make our apologies.

That is how our friendship has evolved over the years. The apology. For the first few years, my wife stated what she would do to adapt or fix things while telling me how garbage I was. You couldn't get her to verbalize an apology to Jesus for her sins. That is one of the greatest changes we have made within our friendship — we both can apologize. Yet, in order for her to be able to do that she had to believe that I could change, she had to feel comfortable enough to be really vulnerable with me.

Looking back, perfecting our friendship has been the key to our success in our marriage. In fact, when I consider all of the factors that make for the foundation of any marriage, I understand that this is the most important one. I also recognize that it is our friendship that has saved us from self-destruction long after the third strike.

Make Mine A Double

by Jennifer Greenberg

My dream job if money didn't matter:
Novelist. But because money does matter.
Pony.
Or first helicopter admitted to Hogwarts.

"Why not all three?" I asked my first-ever Hinge match. Before uprooting to New York that January 2019, I had been a dating app virgin. In Tel Aviv, people met in bars, markets or at the beach over shared smokes and sunsets.

"You are an overachiever, huh?" he remarked over the app's form of messenger. *I guess ponies were within reason.*

"What gave it away?" I asked.

"I have a sixth sense ;) I would ask you on a late-night impromptu date if that weren't weird." *Right to the chase. Bold.*

"It might take me four hours as I'm in New Hampshire," I typed.

"Alright. See you at 2 am!"

Lake Spawford was dead silent, turning the whispers of clicking fingernails against my iPhone glass into screams. While my aunt and uncle slept soundly upstairs, I spent the frigid February night on the basement pullout, playing phone pong with my erudite mystery man.

"Just kidding. I'm free after 4 all week." Spoken like a true 26-year-old liberal arts graduate.

"I mean once you're a novelist you can write drunk edit drunk, isn't that what Hemingway used to say?" I joked.

"Write drunk edit sober," he corrected then one-upped me: "He used to say that *before* he shot himself with his shotgun... he wasn't as garrulous after that."

From dusk to dawn, we argued over Montaigne, Marxism and mania, more starry-eyed than the constellations in New England's untouched sky.

"This banter leaves me unequivocally happy!!!!" I imagined him cringing at the severity of my punctuation.

"Montaigne suggests men are not to judge of our happiness till after death—"

The Wi-Fi crashed as my family woke to the aromas of freshly-brewed Green Mountain coffee, then decided to take the long weekend off. My reply would hang in the balance of an open-ended ellipse.

I returned to New York that Presidents' Day evening to a suggested date and time: "4pm this Fri?"

"Sure, why not?" A nod at nonchalance when, in reality, I felt the least bit composed.

He picked the place: Double Down Salon. *A salon, how romantic.* It was a refreshing break from my obsessive need to control everything. I hadn't met the guy, yet I trusted him more than any family or friend-turned-foe in my newly New York life.

I arrived at 1st and Avenue A in a sweat. My red-black plaid button down and skinny jeans clung to every inch of my being. I hid my unruly Jewish curls beneath a yellow beanie. It had been distinguished in early correspondence through last names and dueling Israel profile photos that both of us were part of the Tribe, which was one of my few dating nonnegotiables. My mother's as well.

"I see Hebrew in one of your pictures," I announced out of thin air, followed by a fast-flow of messages rushing quicker down screen than my racing thoughts.

He found my erraticism quite endearing. "If your writing style is anything like your texting style, I like it… it's manic and lightning fast and gives the impression that you're about to go skydiving." His observation foreshadowed my imminent battle with bipolar disorder. "And yes, I'm Jewish, too, so I love bagels and have a huge... collection of Wiesel's work," he joked.

Expecting to walk into a literary salon, the grimy East Village dive bar took me by surprise. Speedreading as always, I had accidentally omitted an 'O' from the word "saloon." I hoped he hadn't chosen Double Down Saloon for the hard porn shouting over adjacent TV screens, or the tasteful signature shot coined, "Ass Juice." The bar was barren save the blue-haired punk bartender yielding a whip (I did not dare ask why) and a fair-skinned man sporting a red-black plaid and yellow beanie akin to mine.

"Well, this is awkward," I exclaimed, sheepishly noticing our matching uniforms.

He half-smiled and asked, "What's your poison?"

"Double gin and tonic." Who leads with a double on a first drink of a first date?

"Me too." A full smile this time.

I was staring at a mirror into my sullied soul. Was I being punked?

As my date fumbled for an introduction, I wondered if this was truly the charming wordsmith I had fallen for on-screen. He apologized for his slurred speech, having polished off a half-bottle of Jameson prior to the engagement. I was willing to give him a shot nonetheless. After all, I had spent the day rubbing margarita salt in my working wounds at a Mexican restaurant nearby. Two drunk reformed freelancers, oy vey.

My (un)Hinge(d) match carried the chipped lowballs over to the graffiti-tattooed booth, spilling most of their contents onto the uneven floorboards. Shaky hands suggested nerves at first. When he broke the awkward silence with a dramatic monologue about his psychotic break abroad, I understood that his tremors were a side effect of the Lithium, a pill commonly used to treat bipolar mania.

His full-frontal honesty seemed oddly contagious. I let down my guard, donning my penchant for zeniths and nadirs. I received my formal 'Bipolar I' diagnosis later that spring.

"I once got salmonella covering a 4/20 Negev desert festival and instead of going to the hospital, I went into work," I boasted, as if it were an honorable achievement.

"That's messed up. They let you stay?" I sensed the incredulity in his tone.

"Well, they sent me home and insisted I go to the ER. But I felt like superwoman. I completed that month's layout on my bathroom floor clutched to a toilet bowl. Didn't faze me. It was a fabulous feat. And an amazing diet, too.

"The next month, it was my bed I couldn't get out of," I wilted, taking a swig of watered-down Gordon's.

He swirled his melting ice and offered a rebuttal: scored wrists. I saw his self-harm and raised him slashed thighs, following suit with a roulette wheel of eating disorders and inpatient programs. He summered at New York-Presbyterian uptown. Every round of double gin and tonics brought on a new round of confessions, until we were both sauced and bled dry of secrets.

Usually, I put up a front, hiding my disorderly conduct entirely from both prospective suitors and long-term boyfriends. But within half an hour, we knew everything there was to know about one another. The rest was easy. No bombshell too heavy. Except that May, when I cut my 2019 winter fling loose with a clichéd text basically equating to: "It's not you, it's me."

Our three-month relationship had thwarted all truisms. But I wanted to spare his feelings before performing my final monologue: "An Acetaminophen Overdose by any Other Name."

"My hypothesis is that people can only take so much eccentricity before they ghost," he texted back, brutally blasé. It stung worse than the burn of being woken back to life by four EMTs in my Stuytown bedroom. Barely manic and on the brink of a major depressive episode, taking my life with a one-way ticket to the 27-club felt like a befitting birthday present to gift myself. *All's well that ends well.*

My suicide attempt didn't pan out. Neither did our relationship. But he showed up to Mt. Sinai's 6th floor psych ward with gifts: a brand-new yellow beanie, full-liter flask, and wool slippers—in case I felt "sheepish" about the whole ordeal. We split a PB&J and toasted our friendship over a bottle of fine aged apple juice.

One year zipped by since that frenetic February all-nighter. My old flame became my best friend in life. And with much therapy and outpatient programming, I've accepted that it is a life worth living.

"How do you combat the banality of existence?" I had asked him that bitter New Hampshire night. "I've been orbiting the perplexing peripheries of the East Village planet for a few weeks... still so new to the city, it's hard not to feel mundane."

"I'm still trying to conquer that particular existential conundrum," he wrote. "I think once you feel life's banality creeping up on you like a spider on your forearm you've probably already been bitten... and you either turn into Spider Man or die of poisoning."

I'd already ruled out the latter. It was time to channel my inner friendly neighborhood Spider Man.

What Happened When My Boyfriend Became My Girlfriend

by Suzannah Weiss

We tried to love beyond gender, and hit the wall.

On our first OKCupid-initiated date, Ryan* and I timidly gazed at each other across a cafe table, punctuating the silence with sips of lattes. But by the time the discussion escalated to our common childhood spiritual obsessions, it was as if we had known each other forever.

"The Hinduism phase was the best one."

"It really was."

As we got to know each other more over the next few weeks—our Scrabble strategies, our opinions on Lady Gaga's merit as an LGBT icon, and even the darkest revenge fantasies we'd ever had—the awkward silences evaporated. We spent our dates laughing through inconsequential debates like "What does it mean to have your cake and eat it, too?" (He somehow got through 19 years thinking it meant "to serve dual purposes, the way cake is both food and decoration.") During one of our outings, a homeless man asked Ryan for a sandwich and he bought him two.

Less than a month passed before we said "I love you," and the ensuing spring was a whirlwind of covert hand-holding at parties, waking up to roses on my windowsill, five-minute breakups followed by poetic apology notes, and everything else involved with being 20 years old and in love for the first time.

But one aspect of our relationship was not typical — and was not something I thought I'd signed up for.

Ryan had always told me he felt uncomfortable in the male gender role, which I viewed as a positive. At the time, I was reading feminist and queer theory, participating in a discussion group about trans rights, and gaining awareness of how our society's definition of masculinity harms both men and women. A macho man was not for me.

But as time went on, Ryan began dropping hints that his discomfort was more deep-seated than I originally understood. When I'd ask what he was going to do about that, he'd say "I don't know," and I'd get worried, so eventually he dropped it. In my mind, it was no longer an issue. But in his mind, a seed had been planted that was growing larger each day.

One afternoon I got a call from Ryan while I was at the gym. He said he had to see me. Thinking this was one of his romantic surprises, I rushed off the elliptical, back to my dorm and into his arms. But I didn't get the welcoming embrace I was accustomed to.

"We need to talk."
"Are you breaking up with me?"
"We're completely different people."
"But you love me."
"No, I don't anymore."

The rest of that spring semester was the worst period of my life. Every morning, I woke up praying that the inexplicable breakup was just a terrible nightmare. Every waking moment was filled with an ethics lecture on which I wanted his opinion or a talking dog video I wanted to show him or a flower shop where I once got him a tulip after a fight because they were his favorite flower.

In early June, I sent Ryan a card for his birthday explaining how much our relationship meant to me. I hoped this letter would give me closure, along with the physical distance between us as I traveled to Italy to study abroad that summer. But shortly after arriving, I received a Facebook message from Ryan with the following explanation:

I was always an open book with you. But there was one thing I never was able to be as honest as I wanted about. Since I was very young, I felt uncomfortable living as a male. I would ride my bike to Walmart to buy girls' clothing. I felt so ashamed and confused about why I did this. When I was a freshman in high school, I saw a documentary about transgender people. It clicked to me that I was transgender. My parents freaked out and tried to convince me it was a phase. I sunk into a severe depression. In order to just be normal, I acted masculine.

I broke up with you because those feelings were coming back up. I cared about you too much to tell you the truth at the time. I hope you understand that I need to transition to live a happy life and that I do and always will love you. I gave you all of myself when we were together and will continue to do that as long as you allow me.

As I read and reread this last paragraph, the cloud that had been hanging above me over the past few months lifted. The breakup wasn't my fault. He hadn't stopped loving me. I was finally waking up from the nightmare. I called Ryan and immediately suggested we get back together.

The impending transition was an afterthought. We'd cross that bridge when we got there, I figured. After all, I believed sexuality was fluid and love knows no gender and our love, if anyone's, could conquer anything.

But we got to that bridge sooner than I expected. We didn't see each other for the rest of the summer, but if Facebook was any indication, we were a couple—and I couldn't define what kind of couple we were. I was terrified that we couldn't be a couple at all, at least not "forever" like we'd promised each other.

We argued on Skype every few nights about Ryan's transition. I pulled intellectual arguments out of gender theory books to try to dissuade him from going through with the identity change or hormone treatments (he wasn't planning to get surgery). I cited scholar Janice Raymond's assertion that "a female mind in a male body only makes sense as a concept in a society that accepts the reality of both." The very goal of making his body or mode of dress "match" his personality, I said, validated gender norms. Why couldn't he just be a feminine man?

I understood that I couldn't intellectualize away someone's deep-seated identity. But I was afraid of losing him. To what, exactly, I wasn't sure. I'd seen documentaries about people undergoing gender transitions, and they always reassured their friends and family that they would be the same person. But I felt like someone else was about to replace my boyfriend. I felt cheated out of the person I fell in love with.

Even when we tried to talk about other things, Ryan's gender identity was the elephant in the room. I'd constantly beg for reassurance that he wouldn't break up with me over it again. He'd send me messages like: "I'm worried that I'll put a lot into this relationship right now, and when you get home you will realize what I want to do and not want to be with me."

The truth is, I didn't fully grasp what the transition would mean. I had tunnel vision clouded by my fear of losing the most precious person in my life. But when I got home that August, it did get more real.

First, there were little things like wearing nail polish. "I can handle that," I thought. "I know cis men who do that." The next step was wearing women's underwear, which was his way of feeling more like himself without fear of public judgment. (It was unclear what pronoun Ryan preferred to go by. Ryan still presented as a man to most people, but out of necessity rather than preference. And he preferred the label "genderqueer" over "man" or "woman.") That was when I started to feel viscerally repelled.

This repulsion brought me face to face with my own socialization. Whether or not sexual orientation is innate, as the "born this way" argument would suggest, I doubt there's a gene for preferring masculine clothing. After all, I knew from my studies that associations between gender and fashion were culturally specific and arbitrary. I hated myself for letting these arbitrary associations make me averse to my own boyfriend's self-expression. I was an instrument of the gender stereotypes I detested, and they were hurting my relationship. Still, I wasn't going to give up the love of my life over a few pairs of panties, so I reminded myself he was the same person underneath and got used to it.

When Ryan started to buy women's outfits, my distaste turned to panic. I pictured myself walking down the street with someone others would scornfully label a transvestite. I pictured everyone wondering what we were at family gatherings. I couldn't imagine how I would explain. I couldn't image how we would exist.

I wanted my boyfriend back instead of this stranger I had never seen before. But Ryan reminded me that I was now getting more of the person I loved, referring to himself as Ryan 2.0. The new-and-improved Ryan still made snide remarks about the religious right and listened to a baffling combination of gangster rap and country music and bought lobsters just to set them free in the ocean. More importantly, Ryan took more care than ever to remind me that he loved me with thoughtful gestures like making a collage of our love notes for my birthday and bringing me my favorite baked goods when I was stressed out with school. During the rare moments when we were able to take our minds off Ryan's gender identity, I caught glimpses of the untainted relationship I was desperate to preserve.

But more and more alarms interrupted these sweet dreams of how things used to be. Ryan started talking to doctors and therapists about going on hormones, which would cause him to develop wider hips and small breasts. I wondered, would this make

151

me bisexual? Pansexual? I had never been attracted to a woman before, but I couldn't imagine my attraction to Ryan suddenly disappearing. And he didn't want surgery, so our sex life wouldn't be too different. I was braced to at least try to make it work, as I was with the clothing and makeup and everything else that went into the transition.

These changes were even more overwhelming for Ryan. On top of trying to figure out who he wanted to be and how to craft a life that would accommodate that person, Ryan had to deal with a partner whose desires conflicted with the person he was becoming.

Out of the blue one evening that September, Ryan sent me an uncharacteristically angry Facebook message calling me "fucked up" and blocking my Facebook and my number. With no way to contact Ryan, I fell into a state of grief for another two months.

In November, Ryan unblocked me and sent me a message similar to the one from June admitting what I already suspected: "I broke up with you because I knew romantically we could never make it work with what I needed to do." Sadly, this was true. Even though I didn't want to be the one to end it, having that decision made for me was a relief. The constant arguments and uncertainty about the future were causing us both more stress than the relationship was worth. And Ryan still had to sort out a lot of confusion about his identity and find a place to live, line of work and community that would allow for it.

As the dust settled over the course of the following year, we met up a few times as friends. Ryan was on hormones at that point but wore loose, gender-neutral clothing and looked pretty much like the boyfriend I once had. We reminisced about our relationship and agreed that our love for each other would outlast it, even if we lost touch.

We did lose touch over the years, as exes often do. So now, all my information about Ryan comes from Facebook. At one point, she changed her name to something more feminine and her profile photo to one in makeup, earrings, and a homemade poster in the background quoting Lady Gaga: "Baby, you were born to be brave." About a year after this personal rebranding, I was surprised to find that Ryan had switched back to his male name and a photo with a shaved head and masculine clothing. His Facebook wall now contains an amalgamation of *Playboy* photos, graphic anti-abortion campaigns and statuses like "The friend-zone is the only place that has more deflated balls than a Patriots game."

I don't understand. I don't try to.

But my best speculation is that Ryan hit the same wall I did when trying to envision his post-transition life, and bounced back in the opposite direction.

The wall I'm talking about is plastered together with our society's definitions of a man, a woman, a person, and a relationship. You've probably hit this wall, too, perhaps without recognizing it. Women may have hit it when trying to assert their desires in relationships. Men may have hit it when trying to be emotionally vulnerable with their partners. And while it would be so easy to say I was just physically incapable of a romantic relationship with a self-identified woman, I find it more likely that this wall divided Ryan and me from each other and blocked my view of a future between us.

Even now, it's blocking my story from you, the reader, because the right words to describe Ryan and me and our relationship simply don't exist. There's no word for someone who usually lives as a man but feels more like a woman but really is neither or both or somewhere in between. There's no word for the sexual orientation of someone who accidentally fell in love with a woman in the process of falling in love with a man. Instead, I'm forced to leave you with a muddled mix of he's and she's and no answers.

I can only give you questions leading to more questions. I see in hindsight that there were other reasons the relationship didn't work out, including the immaturity reflected in Ryan's "fucked up" message and the ugly side now evident on his/her Facebook wall, but if this weren't the case, would I have let gender confusion ruin an otherwise worthwhile relationship? If I find myself in this situation again, will my increased comfort with gender nonconformity and decreased concern with others' opinions make the relationship easier? How can we tear down the wall that makes such relationships so difficult?

All I can say for sure is that I will always love him, her, or whomever Ryan turns out to be, not as my boyfriend or my girlfriend but as the person who was and still is my first love.

Name has been changed.

Panda With A Gun

by Carolyn Busa

Eats, Shoots and Leaves, the title of Lynne Truss's book on punctuation, has always amused me. I love how the addition of that one, silly comma drastically alters the sentence and what was meant to be a simple fact about a panda bear's diet becomes a comical (and dangerous) situation.

I thought of this book as I sat in bed in the early morning hours of the new year. I had just taken my first sip of coffee in 2020, blissfully unaware of how the year would eventually play out. It was a cup of coffee that I did not make and it was a cup of coffee that I did not request. It was a cup of coffee that, without me knowing, was placed near my face as I slept. It's invisible smell twirled into my unconscious nostrils and then, like a cartoon bear following its nose to a freshly baked pie on a window sill, I woke up sniffing.

In front of me was an outstretched hand holding this cup of coffee in a perfectly shiny, perfectly red mug. It could've been Heaven. Or an IKEA ad.

"What a perfect start to the day, to the year, to the decade!" I thought as I sipped. "I could get used to..." But before I could finish that thought, reality reared her head. She came with the reminder that even though I was in the bed of someone I've known and visited for over a year and a half, this was still a bed that belonged to, a fuck buddy.

Now, I've never been a fan of the term 'fuck buddy'. In fact, I go out of my way not to use it. You don't fuck buddies. You talk baseball with them. Slap them on the back. Buy them a beer. No, I prefer to refer to those I've been intimate with as my lovers. Many people laugh when I do. I think they can't help but hear

Rachel Dratch and Will Ferrell crooning "Lovahs!" in a hot tub. But that's not how I say it. And humor's not my intent. When I talk about "my lovers", I'm not trying to be dramatic or funny. Casual or not, my decision to be intimate with someone is not one I make without some serious thought. My lovers will always be important to me for one reason or another.

Especially this particular lover. Our non-relationship/relationship had been a consistent, surprising, fun, unique, eye-opening and blindfolding good time. It's why I trusted him with my body, with my last hours of 2019 and with my first hours of 2020. But when I received that cup of coffee, my brain took it upon itself to twist the non-relationship/relationship I knew and loved and created what the comma did to the panda bear's eating habits — a dangerous situation.

I had a flash of him waking me up like this every day. Every new year. Living together, being in love, maintaining our odd libidos despite everything working against us. The fundamental differences about us I knew existed suddenly replaced with bullshit We're made for each other scenarios.

"*Fuck, buddy!*" I said to my brain. "Do *not* go there!"

I knew perfectly well our connection wasn't meant for that scenario. We weren't Friends with Benefits that would see the light and finally fall in love in the middle of a flash mob. I knew all this, accepted all this, was happy with all this, and yet for a brief moment my brain wanted to destroy it. "Come on, Carolyn! Make this something bigger. Make this something more!"

Even though it was just a cup of coffee and not a wedding ring, it was still a reminder that despite all my self-proclaimed growth, I was still getting used to simple acts of intimacy and basic kindness coming complimentary with relationships of all kinds, even the casual ones.

It took me quite a handful of lovers to realize just because a relationship is 'casual', does not also make it 'cheap.' "You get what you pay for." is for hotels, not my basic human needs. And hello! Even the Super 8 in Brooklyn provides a little sustenance with their complimentary breakfast.

Treating lovers with kindness and compassion and being treated with kindness and compassion should always be included in the price. Let's remember, we are told a version of this as children, "Treat others as you would want to be treated." Yet when it comes to casual sex, we sometimes lose sight of this, finding ourselves shocked when we actually are treated how we want to be. As if the fact that I have lovers and not boyfriends somehow renders me incapable of caring about comfort, consistency, and communication. But those things and being baseline kind to someone isn't 'going above and beyond.' I'm still a human. I need a blanket when it's cold. I need food when I'm hungry. My goodness, if coffee made me slip for a moment, I fear I would have mistaken an egg and cheese on a bagel for a proposal. "I do! I do! I do... need ketchup!"

I'm glad I didn't let a simple cup of coffee, albeit a damn fine cup of Devoción coffee, completely trick my brain. Questioning what I knew was a perfectly good thing. Sipping and searching for a lifetime romance that would never be. He has exactly one photo hung up in his apartment. I have over 30 in my entrance. It would never work! And that's okay.

Not all relationships need promotions. If your current needs are being met — great! Check! Sold! Set it and forget it! Putting limits on our relationships with others doesn't make the relationship flawed, it makes it honest. Whether it's your Sunday lover or a parent or a colleague, no one should be forced into a role they don't want to or can't play.

If I were to one day want more than a weekly lover who makes good coffee, someone who fills me not only sexually but fundamentally and emotionally as well as someone who fills their walls with as many photos as I fill mine, perhaps then I would reevaluate that relationship.

Because the great thing about being honest in relationships is when you're no longer enjoying yourself, when I'm no longer enjoying myself, it's a lot easier to find the energy to change it. I don't have to sift through facades. I don't have to find myself before I fix myself.

Stopping myself from seeing my Sunday lover simply because we were casually coasting and not seriously progressing would only have been a serious loss. Cutting that relationship out of my life would have denied me pleasure I knew satisfied and filled me. I wasn't leaving his apartment late every Sunday evening lonely and wanting more. No. I was leaving exhausted, fulfilled and grateful that my body was charged for another week. I left feeling powerful. I was the panda with the gun.

Life of Bi

by June Moon

The life of a bisexual, gender fluid, polyamorous individual is precarious. There happens to be lot of other negative words to describe us. Homewrecker is just one of the few. See, we're in an odd predicament. We fit in most places. I can chill with the boys and the boi's. I can kick it with the femmes, stem's, studs and Trans folk. A better word may be chameleon. But plain and simple, I'm also a threat.

Yes, I know you know it and I know it, too. Which is why for the longest time, the "B" in the LGBTIQ(GQGF) was frowned upon or resented. *Choose a side*, we'd hear. If only I *could* choose. In kindergarten, I had a crush on a girl. In first grade, I had a crush on a boy. I had my first girlfriend in third grade. I had my first boyfriend in sixth grade. My bi life goes back like rocking chairs.

Take caution, while I'm kicking it and chilling, it's also in my nature to look cute and flirt.

Let me introduce scenario number one, which I like to call "Unfinished Business Life." I met a new, young celebrity on the rise of success as a musician and filmmaker. She was travelling and performing without her mate. She was fine, and I mean hella *fine*. I couldn't resist complimenting her, her style, and her music. We flirted back and forth. Shit, I'm not the one in a monogamous relationship, even though I claim to have some respect for them. She made me aware of her partner, immediately, because I asked, even going so far as to say she felt guilty talking to me. I understood that feeling. I came forth with all of the compassion and empathy my heart could muster. Yet, I'm hue-man and a prisoner to lust. I gave her my number through Facebook. The next day, unasked, she returned the favor. Here, I must mention, she's a youngster and to communicate, we had a 21st century affair. Meaning, most communication was done electronically. But I romanced the hell out of her with emails, text messages, and Instagram hearts, lmao.

Now, you're trying to find fault. I have to stop you, because I'm also hella fine and extremely charming. I get it from my daddy. All humility out the door, I warned her of my irresistibility. This electric romance was heavy and deep. We shared insanely private secrets in a short amount of time. We connected like, dare I say it… soulmates. It seems cliché until you're in the midst of figuratively standing in unadulterated nakedness. We bared our souls to each other. Weaknesses, silent ambitions, sour addictions, dense childhood memories, high hopes, and big dreams. I asked her to share her innermost wishes as I told her mine. We then sponsored each other on the actualization of those wishes. To me it was like holding a promise for our best self, for each other. Yeah, like that.

We had exactly three phone conversations. Let me go back. I'm a '70s kid. The phone was our link to the outside world. It was how we gauged our popularity even. How many of you remember landlines? We had one line, one phone, and it was in the kitchen. Since my mom wouldn't spring for an additional line, I begged for a long cord. I would test the limits of that cord in the name of privacy while talking to a love interest or making plans to go out on the weekend.

Now getting back to our three conversations. The first one was when we established a romantic interest. The second one, we confirmed we liked each other. The third one was to plan.

Time passed and fate conspired for us to see each other. I thought it was a dream come true when she invited me to her home for the weekend. Conflicted much? Ecstatic to see her and be invited to meet her family, friends, and wait for it, yes, the lover, the partner and in her words, her everything! Now the dread feeling came in. I was sick with nerves. I asked twice, is your partner okay with me visiting? I literally reminded her, "You know we 'like' each other, right?" I questioned, "Have you experienced a new love interest in the same space and time as your current partner?" She replied no. Then I remembered that I had.

It was case number two, which I'll call "Unrequited Love Life." I'm lifelong friends with benefits with a man. He's been my best friend since he was in kindergarten and I was in 2nd grade. Now, let me describe this dude. Tall, handsome, intelligent, warm brown eyes, caring soul, loves his momma and daddy. Helps to take care of his niece who suffers from juvenile diabetes. Steady job, educated, houses (yes plural), nice car, open-minded, and very sweet. All the things. If you can imagine the numerous women that flocked to him and fell at his feet, then you would know how many haters of our friendship there were. Oh so jealous. I've been at his side through elementary, high school, college (we attended universities one mile apart), and girlfriends that numbered in the double digits. Eventually, I fell in love with him also, I mean damn, I have a heartbeat. Then, being witness to the girls became almost painful. Wasn't I the ultimate homie and potential girlfriend? I could chill, be a designated driver, a wingman, and rock him between the sheets. But commitment or becoming something other than besties wasn't in the plans. Over time, and it has been decades, the feeling of wanting more, transformed into a safe and comfortable friendship. I wouldn't take nothing for that, even with all of the angst I used to feel over him.

Case number three, I'll call, "She Gotta Wife Life." I fell head over heels, like love at first sight with this incredibly dope woman. We reconnected after having met once. A couple years had passed, and in the interim, she'd gotten married! I literally ran away from her. I rushed home after our second encounter and dramatically collapsed on my pink yoga mat raging at the heavens. WHY! Why? Is this a cosmic joke on me to keep finding these ultra-attractive mates only to find them hitched to another? A bit of sunshine shone through on this interaction when she mentioned being polyamorous. At the time, I balked. I wanted that special someone for me and me only and vice versa. The gods didn't see it. My philosophy of "one love" was truly being tested. If I really believed in one love, then that love was for everyone right? Right? Let me tell you, I fought tooth and nail against the idea. I felt I was the side bitch, and I wanted to be wifey. I did mention there was already a wifey and time came for us to meet. There I was, sick with nerves. Wait a minute. I recall this feeling...

It was that dastardly weekend when I met the partner. The young lady and I were both shy and nervous about seeing each other again. Mind you, we hadn't seen each other at all in the weeks that had passed since our first dalliance. Would the sparks still be there? Would anyone else see the electricity flashing between us? I had no idea what she told her family about me. I guessed I'd have to play the platonic friend role and oh boy was it difficult. The partner wasn't there yet and I was thanking my lucky stars. This temporary gratitude felt like being underwater. The water feels great, you're having fun, but eventually you have to come up for air. The whole day passed and we were getting to know each other. All was well. Then around midnight, the partner came through the door. I realized in that moment as she gave me a fake ass hug, the true meaning of the witching hour. The tides of what the love interest and I had built turned hard. And not in my direction, not unless the direction led to the exit.

See everything sounds fine in theory. The sophisticated partner may have been like - "Oh, you have a little friend visiting? ... Oh she likes you, huh?" It was all well and good until I was there in the brown, fresh haircut with green hue, eyebrows on fleek, bubble butt in a sport skirt, flesh. Laugh out loud, now honey, but at the time, no one was smiling. It was more so straining. I was completely ignored the rest of the weekend. I kid you not. I was the IG, the invisible girl except to her sister who did a great job of making me feel welcome in an immensely awkward situation. In the end, I was given the digital boot. The last text message I received was, "One day we could be great friends, but not at this time." When I spoke to my homies about the whole story, they told me the potential love interest was likely delivered an ultimatum from her partner. It was her or me, and I was chopped. It took me weeks to gather myself off the dissing grounds.

Last and final case is the case of my barber's interest in me. It's a case I like to call, "Nice Cut, But No Cutty Life." He's heterosexual, cis-gendered, and we share a lot of laughs. Also, he's the one responsible for the extra fresh haircut I had from the first case. He calls it the little Pee-Wee and it's perfectly molded for the shape of my head and the shape of my face. Folks from coast to coast, all genders and colors, have stopped me in the street to complement this look. The first time he gave me this cut, he asked me to dinner. This is one of the perks of the Life of Bi. I get to have double the date opportunity. However, I also get double the diss possibilities, so things balance out. Now, bisexuals are thought by some to be unable to choose a side. More often, we're considered to be straight up freaks. Yeah, that's when all of those tired clichés come in. "Oh, you want your cake and eat it too" lines. I ask you, who of you has had a piece of cake in front of them and won't eat it? I digress. This man just had a newborn baby and was also living with the mother. If we weren't considered freaks, then why in the ham sandwich would he think I'd contemplate such a scenario? Like I said before, I do try to respect relationships. I'm actually not "down for anything." I am, however, down for a free meal, a few laughs, and conversation. Whatever else he had in mind, I had to quickly correct him.

It's true what the sex scientists say, a woman knows within seconds of meeting someone whether or not they're desirable for an intimate tango. My barber is cute and talented, but that electric zap I seek just isn't there. I know the feeling from the first instant I meet anyone either under the Rainbow letters or not, regardless of gender or non-gender and any other possibility of human revelation as it exists in the mind, body, and spirit. The attraction is to the person, period. It's the soul to soul connection that I seek and if I see it in someone, then it is in me to act on it, and that is the Life Of Bi.

My Best Friend's Unintentional Role In my Sex Drive

by Rachel Davies

When it comes to a relationship, sex has always been important for me. Friends of mine have laughed when I say how important, as they talk about trust, intimacy, and humour. For me, however, sex is all of those things wrapped up into one passionate act. I look for all of those other things in partners and, to be honest, without trust and humour and all the other things, the sex isn't that good. It's always been a marker of how much I connect with someone, how strong a relationship is. So when the sex started going downhill with a man I truly loved, it was a world-shattering moment. But then what is 2020 about, if it's not world-shattering moments?

My partner and I moved to Edinburgh from Berlin a week before the UK went into coronavirus lockdown. We both settled into our new flat with relief: glad that we'd made the move, glad that our jobs were both still relatively secure, glad that he, as a German citizen, had even been allowed into the UK during a global pandemic, as borders closed all around us.

Back then, in March 2020, I fully expected COVID-19 to blow over in a few weeks. Being isolated for months in a new city where I knew no one did not even occur to me. But if you had told me then that we would be settling in for months of only seeing each other, I would probably have smirked and made some kind of silly joke about how much time for sex we would have. How wrong I would have been.

By the time COVID-19 looked to be setting in for a long summer, it also became clear that my partner and I would continue to struggle to meet other people in our new city. All the regulation relaxations were designed for people who already had friends and family in the nearby vicinity. The British government announced 'social bubbles', where you could pick another household to have contact with. Somehow I thought my family, living over 400 miles further south, wouldn't be an option. Nor would my partner's family, still a flight away in Berlin.

As our contact with the outside world dwindled, so too did my sex drive. The beginning of lockdown was filled with Zoom pub-quizzes and weekly family hangouts, but our world soon shrank to just the four walls of our sparsely furnished flat. The longer we stayed inside with no one else to talk to but each other, the more our sex life suffered. Sex went from once a day, to a few times a week, to once a week, then even less than that. Sex began to be reserved to drunken nights, and even then we had trouble keeping the reservation.

I wondered (and worried about) if and when my sex drive would pick back up to where it was before. It wasn't just me either; neither of us seemed to have the same level of desire as before. We discussed it openly; there's no room for elephants in the corner when it comes to being locked down in a poky city flat. We both affirmed that all the emotions were still the same, so it wasn't that we were falling out of love — perhaps just out of lust?

Days turned into weeks without actually 'doing it'. We weren't arguing any more than usual and we still cuddled on the sofa before going to bed. My partner and I slipped further and further into an anxious pattern of staying indoors. Even when pubs and restaurants reopened, I found myself too nervous to go out to them and explore the city. This new daily rhythm of nerves and stress didn't leave much room for intimacy.

When chatting in passing about sex drive with a friend, she opened up that she wasn't having as much sex with her cohabiting boyfriend either. "Honestly," she exclaimed. "It's gone down to just once a week." I nodded along, while thinking internally that even once a week was a thing of the past. Apparently, everyone's libido was down — but perhaps not many as far as mine.

As COVID-19 restrictions in the UK began to open up in July, I got the best birthday present imaginable: my high school best friend surprised me with a visit. I had four days of quality time with her, sometimes with my partner as well, sometimes without. In the evenings, I suddenly found a kick to instigate some romance in bed again — not least because he had helped plan the surprise as well. Every night that she was staying in the next room, things were heating up in our bedroom.

Although we had to keep the noise down, we both felt the same passion that we had at the beginning of our relationship. I felt as though I was rediscovering him, but with none of the awkwardness that comes from a new partner. Even when having sex in our favourite and well-practiced positions, it felt like the first time all over again. Nothing had changed and everything had changed at the same time.

Having someone else in our space mixed up the monotonous routine of lockdown. Even after she left, I felt revitalized and freed from the lockdown lifestyle I'd grown used to. Instead of the same 'dinner, TV, bed' schedule that all time outside of work had turned into, we started finding new fun activities to do after work — and not all of them in the bedroom.

We embraced the last few weeks of good weather (something that is easy to miss during a British summer) and explored outside areas of the city that I found on TikTok. Seeing our lifestyle from the outside made me evaluate it myself. My best friend sitting in the flat that had been a refuge for us in the face of the pandemic made me value it all the more. Her questions about what restaurants were good near us woke me up to the fact that we hadn't tried. Put simply, our life as an isolated twosome was put under a gentle microscope. I saw the stagnation for what it was and suddenly found the energy to resolve it.

Moving into autumn now, we've had more visitors come to stay, more dry spells have come and gone, but our sex life has more or less gone back to pre-COVID. Although it's still hard to meet other people close by, travel is easier now, so we can see family and friends more often. My friends have always been important to me and I've always tried to keep a balance in my relationships. Until now, though, I had never realized how integral this balance is to sustaining my own healthy romantic relationship. Having an identity and a social life outside of my relationship is the only way for me to be myself within it. Once I lose my sense of self with my friends, I'm not the same person with my partner.

My partner and I run in a lot of the same social circles, sharing friends as we do everything else. It's not so much time apart from each other that my relationship needs, but the breath of fresh air that the presence of other people can bring. When you're wholly comfortable with someone, as we are together, it's easy to fall into a 24/7 rhythm that seems to fit you both perfectly — until it doesn't.

Maybe it was just the change in routine. Maybe it was having my eyes opened to the less-than-healthy lockdown pattern I was slipping into. Whatever it was, I look back on it now as having a social threesome. Being a serial monogamist, I never would have thought that introducing a third person to the mix would kickstart my libido like it did, but I am immeasurably thankful that it happened.

Gay Rapunzel

by Mike McClelland

I got a summer internship in New York City with one of the world's biggest advertising agencies, Grey Worldwide, in the summer before my senior year of college. It was entirely unearned, at least in terms of experience. My only work experience was digging cremation graves in Greendale Cemetery and working for a few weeks in the antique shop my high school principal Mr. Thresher opened on weekends while he wasn't principal-ing. However, an alumnus of my school, Allegheny College, had gone onto work at Grey and then die tragically and as a result an annual internship was given to an Allegheny student. What I lacked in talent I made up for in ambition (story of my life) and I made sure to kiss the right asses to make sure I'd get the plum New York City job opportunity, a big-deal for a kid from my Podunk hometown.

Through acquaintances, I managed to secure a room in the dormitories of the General Theological Seminary in Chelsea. When I arrived, however, they'd forgotten our arrangement. Being good Christians they offered me a room but the only available space was a converted office on the top floor of the seminary's chapel.

It was a small room, probably one hundred and fifty square feet, with florescent lighting and, thankfully, its own bathroom. The seminarians were kind enough to put a bed from the dormitories and a small refrigerator in the room and reduce the price.

It was perfect. I felt like Rapunzel, an innocent damsel in a high tower in the middle of one of the gayest neighborhoods in the world. The seminary and its buildings were all behind a large wall with a small quiet garden in the middle. I had to enter my room by walking through a big iron gate on West 20th Street, through the garden, into the tall, brick chapel, and up a winding stone staircase to the top floor. It was pure magic.

My windows, wide and metallic in a 1980s newsroom kind of way, looked out over West 21st Street and the immaculate apartment complex across the street. If I leaned out, I could crane my neck and see the Empire State Building.

The internship paid ten dollars an hour, which in New York was just enough to pay my meager rent and buy me ramen noodles and canned vegetables. I spent my spare time running along the Hudson and watching DVDs on my laptop, confined to my room because of a lack of funds.

One July evening, the fading light was hot pink, the kind that comes back as nostalgia years later and bites you right in the heart. Work was an hour's walk and I couldn't afford the subway, so I'd gotten home sticky and smelling of the city. I went for a run along the Hudson, rendering me sweatier and citier, and I took a long shower in my tiny bathroom. I came out into my room, searching for underwear amongst my piles of things (I had no closets) and felt eyes on me.

I swung around. My bed was too low to the ground to be a villain's hidey-hole and I'd just been in the bathroom so the only place to look was out the window. Sure enough, there was a man at the window across the way, staring at my nakedness.

I hit the floor in modesty, relieved that I was not, at least, instinctively slutty. I crab crawled across the floor, back into the bathroom, which had no window. I waited there for what felt like an eternity. When I came out, the man was no longer there, his curtains closed.

Of course, being bored and twenty-one, exhibitionism quickly blossomed. I made sure to shower the same time each evening and within a few days I caught him again. He was handsome. Tall and thick haired. I couldn't believe how close he was. The New York streets felt even narrower up high than they did below.

It began innocently. I let him watch me dress. My head was shaved so I couldn't do any stripper hair flips, thank God, but I did perhaps get a bit too into drying off. Still, it felt entirely innocent. Well, pretty innocent. There was no harm in him watching.

It didn't stop there, though. After a few weeks of him watching me towel off, I came out of the bathroom to find him naked, too. Again, my urge was to hit the floor, but I was frozen in place by the thought that it would be rude. Here he'd been politely watching me for quite some time, I felt obligated to return the favour.

I would have found him much more attractive at my current age, but to my young self he was too old to be my type, probably in his late forties. Already in my young gay life I'd had a difficult time with older men being too forceful. Also, and I say this without armchair psychologist condescension, I had a wonderfully normal relationship with my own father and it made me incredibly uncomfortable when anyone approached me with a "daddy" demeanor.

Still, the across-the-street distance felt safe, and he wasn't demanding. He kept doing inquisitive, tentative thumbs up motions to see if I liked certain things or not. He was, by far, the most considerate lover I'd ever had.

That's how it started and it blossomed into a lovely relationship based on smiles, waves, and mutual masturbation. There was no expectation, though I did find myself glancing at the window waiting for him to get home and open the curtains.

He had a live-in partner and I'd gotten a boyfriend (miraculously, since I couldn't afford to go out for more than one happy hour drink a week). However, his partner always seemed to work late. And my boyfriend, Jeff, was super religious and struggling with his sexuality, making my holy domicile too stressful for him to visit. Though our interactions were strictly above the belt, he wanted to keep even those out of the view of the Lord.

I was the opposite. I saw my Rear Window romance as a gift from God. It was fun and lacked the pressure of other relationships, particularly my relationship with Jeff. I loved that it was so silent, based on convenience, and completely visual. As a youngster and teenager I struggled mightily with my looks and weight, so what a thrill to be wanted only for my looks.

Even as my interactions with the guy across the way became bolder, I resisted trying to meet him in real life. I made sure to never walk down West 21st Street, for fear I'd run into him outside his building. Once, he held up a paper with his phone number, and I shook my head. I wasn't ready for that.

So we stayed as we were. It didn't lose its thrill, which was a shock. Everything thus far had lost its thrill. Over the course of two months my relationship with Jeff had curdled from new and exciting to a source of constant anxiety. Still, I kept it going until the end of my time in New York.

I didn't feel as if I was betraying Jeff with window guy, though I'm not sure why. And I didn't feel like window guy was cheating on his partner. But we weren't just friends, either. We weren't friends at all. We were lovers. I knew the look of his body better than anyone I'd been with before. We couldn't be together in the dark. He taught me what I liked about a man. I thought I'd known, but so much of that is based off what a man can do for you with his body. Looking is entirely different.

Jeff liked to go be fancy in the Hamptons on the weekends and for my last weekend in New York I accompanied him. We'd been talking about staying together, about me moving to New York after I graduated college the following year. Then, on a beach in Sag Harbor, the least classy of Hampton's locales, Jeff told me that God didn't want us to be together, depriving me of the Hollywood moment putting up with Jeff had earned me.

I knew that was a lie. Not because my line to God was stronger (though it was; God and I had a very happy relationship whereas Her's and Jeff's was rather fraught), but because I could see it in his eyes. Jeff didn't want me the same way the man in the window did.

I got the bus back to New York. My parents were coming

to pick me up and take me back to college the next day. I started packing up my few belongings. I kept checking the window, waiting for the man in the window to appear, even though it was a Sunday and him and his partner rarely opened the curtains on weekends.

I was weeping like a fool because that's what you do when someone dumps you and shoving piles of clothes into garbage bags. I went and took a shower, washing the bus off of me, and when I came out I looked across the street again, as was my routine. And there he was.

It was only then that I wondered if something happened when I showered. Maybe the tops of my room's windows fogged, or some pipe on the side of the church blew steam out. The water just went into a hole in the bottom of my shower; perhaps it just flew out into the street?

Regardless, he was there. Clothed, but with his dick out. Which was flattering in its own way. He held up a piece of computer paper with "Leaving? ☹"

Naked, I nodded.

For the first time, he held his hand up and beckoned. Come here, his hand said.

I shook my head. I was too nervous. Even though I felt I knew him, I didn't want to go into a stranger's apartment in New York City. I was still, at heart, a small town boy.

He frowned and then held the paper up again. "I can come there. ☺"

He smiled as he put it up, and I smiled as I caught the double entendre.

The nerves were still there, but this was a chance I wanted to take. As I was already on the top floor of the church, I shot a little prayer to the Empire State Building, and, having no ladder of hair to throw out the window, wrote my number on a piece of paper and held it up to the window.

Self-Destruction In the Name of Black Love

by Aitza Burgess

Despite my liberal, sex-positive upbringing, I'd deluded myself into becoming someone whose sexual satisfaction was of little importance. In the quest of being the ideal Black woman, worthy of Black Love, I stopped being a person who maintained the belief that being a healthy and happy woman meant my sexual fulfillment was nonnegotiable. I kept participating in gender roles I didn't believe in. Finding myself engaging in sexual acts that brought me little to no gratification. I justified it because my research had worked. The pain I endured wasn't for a lost cause. In the rat race of dating the finite pool of Black men who dated Black women, I had succeeded. Now people would think twice before questioning my loyalty to my race.

But let me give you the background on how I arrived there…

I'm a Black American woman who knows that I'm attractive and beautiful. It's something I'm not shy about. It has resulted in me being called vain. I have an aesthetic that fits within the European mode of object beauty: Being of thin, athletic build with long legs and a petite stature. It is a physique that comes with several privileges.

My proximity to beautiful, as defined by the white male gaze, makes my life easier even with darker skin. I can navigate certain spaces, knowing I will be treated as if I possess a type of femininity and beauty that are valued. But this specific aesthetic is not heralded within my own racial and ethnic communities. I don't have the physical features that an objectively beautiful woman of African descent is supposed to have. Under the Western gaze and media reinforcement, which is controlled and dominated by white people, Black women have been fetishized and dehumanized for centuries. Instead of viewing us a people, we are reduced to caricatures: full lips, large breasts, and a big ass. To be objectively beautiful with dark skin, one must have those features. One with a body type like mine, the stereotype says that I should have lighter skin, brighter eyes, and looser curls.

These narrow, constrictive categories of beauty shaped the framework for what a real Black woman is supposed to look like. And it often acts as a form of currency in the dating and sex market with Black men. Through various forms of entertainment, the message has been made clear. In order to gain Black Love in America when you look like me, means that you have to release agency in exchange for submission, endure romantic suffering, or alter your image to fit the prized physical aesthetic; that of the perfect Black woman with large breasts and a big ass.

No matter how much you love yourself, being deemed unattractive by your own racial group and constantly feeling undesired by those who look like you eventually is a massive blow to your self-esteem, especially when your culture conditions you to only want and seek Black Love. When society has told you that your worth as a woman is tied to men seeing their own beauty reflected in you, it's as if it becomes your duty to fulfill that moral obligation.

For me, part of fulfilling that obligation meant denying non-Black men access to me and the love that I have to offer. Many people regard dating interracially, as a Black woman, as a negative cultural mark. This is often expressed as "*I think that I am too good for Black men and don't want to give them a chance.*"

It's more than just dating or sex. It becomes about the survival of Black American culture and your ability to sustain it. That's how you get closer to the fairytale version of Black Love that has been sold to you. The one American media has made devoid of the greater force that Black partnerships and marriages have been in the US for centuries. Like any fairytale, you want to live out that fantasy.

Sometime during university, it got back to me that I was seen as one of those Black women who thought that she was too good for Black men. In reality, my dating non-Black men was circumstantial and purely a numbers game. The gender ratio was 2:1. When you account for the LGBTQ community and those already in relationships, I was no longer in a sea but a small pool of potential partners. If I wanted to have a romantic relationship or sex life, it was to my benefit to consider non-Black men. Living in a sea of whiteness, I wanted to be embraced by my Black peers. A negative cultural marker was not going to aid that community building. Unity and community, like the Black Love portrayed in media, came with terms and conditions, and it was up to me if I wanted to agree to them. And I did.

Hours went into researching the Black couples in my area. I studied my Black female peers' dating profiles. From there, I curated the perfect dating profiles. The music I chose as my favorite songs, how my hair was styled in photos, and the TV shows I mentioned were purposeful. All tailored to reflect something similar to the ideal Black woman and increase my odds. I had no desire to change several physical traits, like my skin tone, hair texture, or breast size. But I could and did want to change the size of my bottom. It was something I became obsessed with. I desperately wanted a Black girl booty that would make Black men flock and stare as I danced in the club. I wanted to be the one who twerks on them. To achieve this, I knew I'd have to endure a bit of suffering.

You see, there's one thing that makes me pack on the pounds: dairy. It's also the thing my body detests the most. I am severely lactose intolerant. To the point where if I don't take the proper dosage of medicine, my insides feel as though they are being ripped apart and repeatedly stabbed until the toxins leave my body. Because that's what lactose is for me — a toxin.

Like many Black women before me, I endured the pain. I sucked up the bloating and gas and occasionally stomach aches. And I enjoyed my goat cheese with honey and thick berry cheesecake milkshake made from an entire slice of cheesecake. If I was going to poison my body, my taste buds would benefit. I was living the life! — until I was bent over the toilet, fighting back the tears and begging God to make the unbearable pain go away.

As I managed the physical repercussions, I ignored the destruction of my true self. During the process, my beauty was dictated by the preferences of men. Men who fetishized me and had been conditioned to accept a distorted view of what Black womanhood was. The worst part being I became an active participant in my own objectification and fetishization.

Everyone in my community had warned me to be wary of romantic or sexual advancements from non-Black men because they would fetishize me. Fear was always spread about how these non-Black men would obsess over my darker skin and the thought of having sex with a "wild" Black girl. But no one warned me that the Black men would also perpetuate these stereotypes. This behavior was part of our intra-racial social contract.

I was not prepared for the reality that some of the men in my community would be focused on my full lips and spend too much time thinking about my ability to suck dick. Or those who saw my dark skin as an invitation to make my body their playground. A place that once they had their fun, caring little for my satisfaction or active and passive participation, they would leave me to couple up with women lighter skinned than the both of us. I was supposed to accept all of this in silence.

I was self-sabotaging my sex life and personal growth. Displaying a "Do not disturb" sign to all non-Black men because they wouldn't help me achieve Black Love. I kept building this version of myself: the version which was swiping on Black men that were and weren't my physical type because looks aren't everything. My true self, the one screaming "This limited pool of men isn't your only option," urging me to stop ignoring the lack of chemistry, the absence of shared ideals, the deprivation of enthusiasm, I locked it away. It would only hinder my quest of living out the fantasy.

That is not to say that all of the interactions were unpleasant. Sometimes you simply don't click with a person, but you know you could be friends. Those are the ones I remember with fondness. Those are the ones I wish had worked because despite there being a dearth of physical chemistry, they saw me as a human and got a peek at my true self. If I could have developed a romantic relationship with one of them, it would have made the times I forced myself to waste hours on dates that lead nowhere worth it.

But those were rare gems. Most saw me as nothing more than an ornament. And it was frustrating. As much as I wanted to fulfill this cookie-cutter role, I also wanted a partner that enticed sexual confidence out of me. What didn't invoke confidence was having my sexual desires dismissed as a sign of whiteness. Being gaslit and told Black men didn't perform certain sexual acts, and no one had complained before, so why should I? There was a point where I was almost being slut-shamed for my vanilla suggestions of being the recipient of oral sex, proposing positions that weren't doggy and missionary, and sharing my sex dreams. All the while listening to a contradictory mindset where they would regurgitate all of the sexist and racists stereotypes about dark-skinned Black women, and expecting me to live up to them. To prove my loyalty to them and, by proxy, our community. If I fulfilled that labor and was publicly linked to them, the shameful marker would be removed from me.

Just as those men were my ticket to the possibility of Black Love and community acceptance, I was their sex toy. Something there to ensure they reached their orgasms. There was little concern about mutual satisfaction. Nothing sent a message that my pleasure was unimportant, other than a few lazy, clumsy swipes across my

179

clitoris. Those careless swipes were insurance that, yes, they did reciprocate oral as they claimed. It was not about experience, but a guarantee that their penis would find a temporary home in a warm, wet spot to repeatedly enter. It is what was expected under the idea that dark skinned Black women are rigidly strong, hypersexual, and made to please Black men. We are supposed to remain silent about our lack of enjoyment and subjugation as long as we're boosting the self-esteem of Black men.

I craved encounters where I got to know my partner's brain first. The ones who were daring enough not to break eye contact and ask profound questions that slowed down my ever racing mind in amazement. Conversations that would leave me wanting to peel off each layer of clothing because of their inability to hide their sheer enjoyment over a new documentary or their favorite author is such a turn on. The kind of interactions with a partner who has made it undoubtedly clear that learning more is a top priority, and that trait would translate into the bedroom.

How I missed phone sex and sexting that was imaginative in a way that was exquisitely painful and deliciously pleasurable. Where there were positive expectations associated with the build-up. Where it wouldn't be the kiss of death to say I fantasized about having my partner slide his cock between my legs, rubbing the head through the wetness. How I envisioned myself moaning when he'd pulled back, stopping his delicious torture by pressing his cock inside me. And nothing was stopping me from having it but this false notion of racial loyalty tied to an unhealthy version of love.

A loyalty that is not only patriarchal but unrealistic. My Black womanhood didn't begin and end at my ability to date a Black man. According to US Census data, there are 88 black male adults for every 100 black female adults in America. Even if every Black man and woman was straight and only partnered with Black people, there still wouldn't be enough Black men to equally pair off. The facts which are missing from the grand narrative of Black Love as marketed in America states the fairytale isn't attainable for all. Yet, many other Black women and I are punished in our community for this gender imbalance. Our Blackness is questioned for it. If my pleasure was not a priority and reality contradicts the story I bought into, why was I there?

Buying into the Black Love or bust narrative was a sacrifice that was too much to bear. It is an unfair expectation to have of myself. Feeding my mind the false tale that I had to cling to the idea of being loved by and only with a Black man was as toxic as the dairy products I put into my body. Ignoring qualitative and quantitative data, which told me I could exist just as I was and still have happy and healthy sexual and romantic relationships was shredding apart the person my pro-Black parents spent so many years molding with love — a person I loved.

And I grew tired. Tired of morphing my body into something it wasn't created to be. Tired of demonstrating this extreme level of physical and mental level chasing after men when I knew I had other possibilities. Tired of dating being something I dreaded, instead of a fun possible romance filled activity. Tired of being hypersexualized. Tired of knowing true Black Love isn't what the media depicted it to be. I knew dating didn't have to be this way. I knew sexual encounters didn't have to be this way. There were men who wanted to take me to dinner, spend afternoons at museums with me, and learn about my interests beyond surface-level factoids anyone who followed me on social media would be privy to.

Many things snapped me out of this self-destructive cycle. But the most riveting was an Audre Lorde quote I saw while mindlessly scrolling social media: "If I didn't define myself for myself, I would be crunched into other people's fantasies for me and eaten alive." I had been allowing others to define me to a point where I was only a shadow of my true self. My parents raised me to know I was worthy, complete, and sufficient as I was. That as beautiful and revolutionary as being with a Black man can be, the fairytale version of Black Love does not define the core of who I am. Whether I found love with a Black man or a non-Black man, only I could express my Black womanhood. Black Love or an attraction from Black men was never the ultimate decider of my self worth and value in life. I needed to return to that mindset.

When I began deconditioning myself from those tight societal conditions of what beauty and Blackness must be for Black women, my relationships and sex life improved. The stakes of saying the wrong thing and subsequently losing access to this person who had been hyped up as the ultimate prize was gone. No longer was there a tension created by a power imbalance, preventing me from expressing that I didn't want sex to happen to me. I was able to talk to my partners and figure out what turned us both on. There wasn't a cultural script that I was expected to perform. The absence of expectation was imperative in finding ways to shut out white noise and focusing on pleasure.

All the Weight Is Not Yours

by Jeana Jorgensen

"I'm becoming a tree wizard," my atheist boyfriend told me on the phone, shortly before he was admitted to the hospital for a psychotic break. This was not the first time, nor the last, that a partner's unmanaged mental illness had intruded on a relationship; another time, I only realized I should leave an unstable partner after he wrecked my car.

I'm not writing this to throw stones, to disparage people with mental illnesses or who are neurodivergent, or to say that people struggling with these issues cannot possibly have healthy relationships. I have high-functioning anxiety, so I'd be hypocritical as well as prophesying a gloomy sex life for myself. Rather, I want to reflect on how much of my partners' struggles I absorbed in past relationships and why I'm resolved not to makes those same mistakes again.

Take the past partner who was hospitalized. He was having a rough streak: had recently lost his job, was reevaluating his life, and so on. He decided to try out a polyphasic sleep cycle (for those not in the know, it means rather than sleeping once through the night – a monophasic sleep cycle – you would instead break your sleep into small chunks, spread throughout the day and night, to give you more wakeful time. I do not recommend it; there's a reason why sleep deprivation is among the tools of torturers worldwide). Between the sleep deprivation and the use of substances ranging from marijuana to psychedelics, he simply lost touch with reality.

When I went to his apartment to get a few things to bring him in the hospital, there was writing on the walls. There were forks stuck into the walls. I didn't know how to reconcile the person who would do these things with the person who I'd begun dating: intelligent, caring, curious.

After some time, he was released, with a prescription for antipsychotic drugs and a bunch of recommendations to get back on track (including ditching illicit substances). I supported him through that, as he got a new job and adjusted to the new patterns in his life. Besides, what kind of partner would I be if I ditched him in his time of need? (I blame feminine socialization for that one; women are conditioned to be giving above all else, often to the detriment of our own needs.)

When it happened again, I still stayed. Looking back, I wonder why, and the only two answers I can come up with are that I was already pretty invested in the relationship and that I thought I couldn't have too high of standards for a partner's mental health, given that mine was already fraught. These two reasons, of course, are intertwined: I had accepted that perhaps I was deserving of substandard treatment, that I could cope with a partner's substance abuse and mental health struggles, because it was part of the whole package of trying to find someone who would love and accept me as I was, flaws and all.

After all, my anxiety sometimes gave me panic attacks. It made me overwork myself to the point where I had small breakdowns and grew physically ill. When it manifested as social anxiety, it paralyzed me when trying to make phone calls, for fear of talking to a stranger while utilizing social conventions that were foreign to me. I was and remain pretty well-adjusted, all things considered, but I had early on internalized the message that I was fundamentally broken, and I'd be lucky to have someone commit to being with me.

So I stayed in that relationship, even as that partner began to verbally abuse and gaslight me about my anxiety (and its occasional friend, depression). Apparently, it was at the root of so many of our relationship problems; when my libido dipped due to depression, it was my fault that we weren't having sex as often. This didn't have to be a huge problem, as we were ethically non-monogamous; however, I also needed to be "nicer" to his other partners, despite me being an introvert needing a lot of alone time to recharge. Further, my anxiety apparently made me too risk averse, which constrained the sexy adventures he felt he could have with other people.

He began to smoke pot again, which worried me given its role in his previous dissociative break. And I chose not to partake with him because that substance does not make me feel good, he felt shamed by my abstinence from it, and cited my anxiety as a problem once more (if only I would quit worrying about what he was doing with his substance use, somehow things would be better between us?). When we'd see each other after his therapy appointments, he would smoke out to numb those emotions and cry (to his credit, since toxic masculinity does awful things to men) while telling me about what was going on with him. However, somehow it was my fault for not wanting to have sex with him after these sessions, because it was not reinforcing his attempts to take care of himself and do the right thing.

These disrespectful things had to keep adding up before I would finally exit that relationship. After all, my anxiety made me a pain to be with; I'd internalized that message during my time with this partner, so if he had his own quirks, well, so did I. No one in this fucked-up world has a perfect mental health record, so how could I hold anyone to an impossible standard? What I missed in that relationship was how my mental health struggles were weaponized against me. Afterward, I resolved not to let that happen again.

I found someone lovely and trauma-informed to date, but within a year, I spotted a familiar pattern: it's not that he was wielding my anxiety against me, thankfully, but rather that he let his mental health go…and I still stayed. This was not all his fault, of course; we were living in a city where having a car was necessary to get around, and once his broke, his options narrowed. Once poverty and joblessness came knocking at his door, his options continued to thin, winnowing his world down to a depressing haze of foreclosed futures. Those problems were systemic, created by the worst-possible version of capitalism that we're currently stuck with. But those problems exacerbated the mental health issues and vice versa, and I helplessly watched, stuck in the script that I should stay in an increasingly-dysfunctional relationship because I found someone who would accept me, anxiety and all. Soon our relationship was a shell of what it once was, with our nights increasingly sleepless (something that gave me bad memories of my other partner's sleep deprivation failed experiments) and our time together less and less intimate.

I had a decent job at the time and spent a lot of nights at his place, so I helped pay his rent a few times. I had the experience with types of writing he wanted to do, so I helped with some of those projects as well. I had a twenty-year old car that was on its last legs, so I loaned it to him once my dad helped me find a replacement for daily driving. My hope was that my partner could get a job, and pay his own rent, and work on his issues, and so maybe it would be worth my staying in that relationship.

Instead, he wrecked my car, couldn't pay rent, and had to leave town. I had to make my peace with how my attempt to stay and be supportive didn't, ultimately, end up mattering in a relationship that was rife with dysfunction due to unaddressed mental health issues. The last few months – if I'm being honest with myself, the last 6 months – of a year-plus relationship were unhappy ones for me, yet I was invested in enough to stay, since I felt accepted and yearned for that stability.

I should not have stayed in either relationship for so long, but past-me had lower standards due to the stigma that accompanies mental health issues. Plus, the sex was good (until it wasn't).

These issues recur in my life: one more story. Once upon a time I felt horrified and violated when one partner casually said they'd been talking with our friends about the possibility that I was on the autism spectrum because my behavior is outwardly weird at times. While there's no shame in such a diagnosis, I was shocked that my partner at the time thought this was a topic to casually converse about with mutual friends. I replayed how these conversations might've gone in my head, feeling fundamentally betrayed at how my quirks (like wanting super direct agreements and boundaries – how is that a bad thing?) became conversational fodder for playing therapist.

Ultimately, I still struggle with finding the balance between wanting a healthy relationship and having unrealistic standards. After all, no one has a perfect mental health track record, me included, and the current structure of the American economy perpetuates inequality and makes it ever-easier for people who are already struggling to be swept further into poverty (and be blamed for their own fates to boot). What I have learned, though, is that what matters is acknowledging and managing one's mental health issues, whether through therapy, medication, building communities, and so on, rather than downplaying and ignoring them. Or, worse, trying to blame your partner for them. I'm definitely on the lookout for that one now, thanks to my past experiences, though they have also left some scars.

Threesome

by Stephanie Conway

I read *Fear and Loathing in Las Vegas* once and loved the idea of living a Pete Doherty-esque lifestyle on the road as an artist, evading the tedious inevitabilities of life through psychedelics and exploration. But my life couldn't have been further from that: I had a corporate career, paid my taxes, and did everything I could to stay cool in my group of competitive LA friends. Not something Hunter S. Thompson would be proud of. So when I met the man who embodied the word 'escapism', I knew I was in for a wild ride.

Andy. He was this skinny olive-skinned man with big googly eyes and jet black hair. He told me he was an artist, and I was blind-sided by his ADHD energy. He was eight years older than me but looked and behaved like he was 8 years younger. I should have known that Burning Man festival wasn't the optimum place to find a boyfriend. You can't expect to have a logical relationship when you go for someone who has frazzled their brain one too many times on acid. I mistook his ADHD for excitement and creativity.

Andy's talents included being an awful bass DJ, laughable writer, sub-par rapper, enfant-terrible painter, and embarrassing breakdancer. He was a cocktail of mortifying levels of non-talent, desperately clamoring for fame as he gradually aged towards his forties. You might find him performing windmills on a dirty dance floor at parties, and I'd usually be trying to find where he had dropped his keys. But I overlooked his hobbies because he was exciting. He also took me to fun events, often brought me flowers, and showered me with affection. We were smitten with one another. I once heard him describe me to his brother as his "ride or die." That was quite a statement about someone he hadn't been with for very long. But it did seem like he loved me almost as much as he loved himself.

Andy lived in the shadow of his wealthy drug lord brother. When his brother did something, Andy always wanted to do the same. His brother had a threesome. So Andy decided that he was going to have a threesome, regardless if I, his girlfriend, wanted to join in or not.

This unrequited threesome decision happened to coincide with a trip that we had booked to go home to visit my parents in the UK, followed by a brief few nights in Iceland on the way home to the US. I had paid for the trip on my credit card, as Andy only dealt in cash because although he told everyone that he was a professional artist, he really made his money cutting the leaves from marijuana plants at his brother's weed farm. You know, the type of work that at the time was cash in hand, untaxed and illegal. So as the only law-abiding citizen of the relationship, naturally I had to pay and he promised to give me cash for his portion. "We'll meet a girl in Iceland and go for it there," he mused. "A threesome doesn't have to happen with two women, it could also be with two men, you know" I prodded. "Ew, not a man. That's disgusting. It has to be a woman.""Okay fine, obviously that's your fantasy but I'm not having a threesome. I don't feel comfortable." He didn't hear me. Whenever I said anything he didn't like, the words would fall on deaf ears.

We arrived in the UK just before Christmas. When meeting my parents for the first time, Andy gave them a print of one of his pieces of modern art. "That'll look good in the garage," my dad said facetiously. After a few days of my parents exchanging choice looks with one another as Andy spoke about his various creative endeavors and plans to become famous, we set off for Iceland. On the plane, Andy started with the threesome craic again. "We'll find a hot blonde girl." "No, we won't, Andy. I'm not doing it." "Yeah, you'll like it, babe!" He laughed as I rolled my eyes and turned to stare out of the window into the darkness.

We spent a few days exploring the magical landscape of southern Iceland: fjords, geysirs, black sand beaches, and picture-perfect cottages nestled against a dramatic sweeping landscape of ancient volcanoes and snow-covered mountains. We were surrounded by so much natural beauty that I had forgotten Andy's ulterior motives. On our last night in Iceland, we went for dinner at a restaurant that featured whale blubber and penguin on the menu. We toasted to the beauty of Iceland over local Brenninvin schnapps. "Tonight's the night, it's now or never," Andy announced. "For god's sake, Andy. Give it a rest." Andy quickly changed the subject but then kept ordering more schnapps and we both began to get quite tipsy. After the meal, we wandered into a nearby bar.

Inside, we got chatting to a mixed group of travelers and locals. "I've always wanted to live in Los Angeles!" A beautiful blonde Icelandic angel overheard Andy's accent. "I'm a singer, so I'd love to go over there to record my music." "Oh really, you're a singer? I'm a music producer. Maybe we could connect and I can make some beats for you," Andy stared into the girl's eyes as if I didn't exist. Her eyes lit up as though she had finally found her ticket to stardom. But she hadn't. If Andy could make her famous, he would have made himself famous first. Granted he did have an app on his MacBook that could make songs, but he definitely wasn't making any money from it. I cook dinner every now and then, but I don't go around telling people I'm a master chef. I turned away from their chemistry and chatted with two off-duty air hostesses about their next flight plans. Andy kept buying both myself and the Icelandic angel rounds of drinks, and I descended into a drunk state. The bar closed and our mixed group walked out into the icy darkness, thinking we would go back to the air hostesses' room for a party. The group broke into two and the Icelandic angel, Andy and I found ourselves lost from everyone else. We decided to head back to our room.

"Can I sing for you?" The angel broke out into her best audition piece for the man who would make her a star. When she had finished, Andy broke into rapturous applause. "Wow! You're a star!" He gushed. I suddenly started to feel sick, unsure if it was the alcohol or the situation. "I'm going to bed." I left the room and went to sleep. I woke up the next morning with two naked bodies cuddling in the bed next to me. The bodies belonged to Andy and the angel. I was so stunned and hungover that I couldn't speak.

"Babe, just get over it. When we go away we can have fun, but when we come home, it's like nothing happened," Andy's wide eyes bulged out of his face as he tried to find the check-in desk. I trembled in fury, but I was too hungover and emotional to say anything clever. We were in Reykjavic airport waiting for our flight back to Los Angeles. In all of the commotion from the night before, awkward morning breakfast with the angel and quickly packing to leave, we had checked-in late and had to be seated separately. I had been placed in the first row next to an off-duty pilot who kindly listened to my emotional recount of last night's events while his unimpressed wife carefully eyed up our conversation from a nearby aisle.

When we touched down in Los Angeles, I had finally recovered from my hangover enough to speak. "You cheated on me!" I cried. "Well, it wouldn't have been cheating if you had joined in," Andy shrugged. Technically, his hypothesis wasn't wrong. If I had somehow woken up and joined in, we would have been having a threesome. But he had overlooked one thing: threesome etiquette. Sex of any kind must be consensual. In no way had I ever consented to the threesome, nor him having sex with another woman at all. So, yes, sure, it could have been a threesome in the same way that if Jason Momoa had miraculously knocked on the door that night and also joined in it could have been a foursome. But he didn't and it wasn't.

I felt betrayed. Betrayal is a weird experience because it only ever happens with someone that you love. But that love didn't last. The day we flew back to Los Angeles, my love for Andy transmuted into disbelief that he could humiliate me so effortlessly, which gradually developed into pure hatred. If I could pinpoint when that hatred arose, it might have been when I received my credit card bill with a reminder that I had paid for the rounds of drinks to get the angel drunk with my credit card. I had also paid for the room for him to cheat on me in - and their shameless breakfast the next morning. He humiliated me, and I picked up the tab. The relationship was dead. But I was trapped. I lived with Andy. We had a dog together. We had joined our living situation, our friends, our lives. It wasn't as simple as just leaving, and Andy knew it. "Hey, we're home now. I've already said sorry, let's move on," he tried to reason, as though my emotions were somehow invalid and irrational. You really can't reason with crazy. I know because I've tried.

So for a while, life went on as normal. We both went back to work, and stayed in the same house together. But I wasn't the same person. I certainly wasn't his "Ride or die." Maybe if this had been the 1950's and I was his dependent housewife, after a situation that we had been through I might have stayed. But I had my own job, and although before we had left for Iceland he had started his own marijuana grow-operation in our rented garage, promising that "it would pay our rent so that we could save for our future." He raked in over $19,000 per harvest, but then decided last minute that I would still have to pay my half of the rent so that he could use more of the money on renting a fancy art studio to paint more of his shit art that no one wanted. So much for investing in our future.

Meanwhile, I lived in a house where I could be arrested at any moment if his operation was discovered. He made sure that any money I had, I made by myself. Up until Iceland, I had overlooked this decision, but now I certainly wasn't his "ride or die." No self-respecting human would be after an Icelandic experience like that. But Andy behaved like nothing had happened. Friends would ask how our trip was, and he would talk about the beautiful landscapes, but I remained silent. All I could think about was waking up to his naked body wrapped around someone else. I needed to get out. So, I booked a trip to Bali. My excuse was that I was going on a yoga teacher training retreat, but I also told everyone that I was leaving for good. No one believed me, not even Andy. I began to get rid of my wardrobe. I put my notice in at work. I said goodbye to my friends, and I left. I left slowly and methodically, and he didn't stop me because he didn't believe me.

"How could you be so selfish and abandon me? I'm so lonely without you!" Andy sobbed over the phone shortly after I landed in Denpasar airport. He couldn't believe I had left. I couldn't believe I had left. All I knew was that I hated him with every ounce of my soul for what he had done. "I'm sorry you're lonely, but I did say I was leaving, you just didn't listen." "It's not just you. I'm going to travel the world too, Steph. I'm just going to wait till I get big and someone pays me to do it." He hung up.

We didn't communicate except for when he would occasionally send me links to his latest artistic creations that I wouldn't ever click on. I didn't hear from him properly until a year later. I received a barrage of drunken messages one evening. "You don't care about me but I still love you. I just want you to know that I learned from this experience. You abandoning me really hurt but I'm stronger now - AND I have a girlfriend. We're happy!" I went on Instagram to verify his claims. From his photos, it looked like he had gained a lot of weight since I had last seen him. He also had photos with a pretty brunette girl. His new girlfriend. They seemed happy and all I could think was; "Good for them."

No Longer Terrified to Be Myself
by Wil Williams

It was during the plague year 2020 that I decided to uproot ten years of a loving, beautiful relationship and subject myself to touch starvation, complicated interpersonal dynamics, and a forced sense of powerlessness. I know how it must look from the outside. 2020 has been a year of downward spirals for most of us, and I'm not exempt, between cutting my bangs in a fugue state to several consecutive days spent in bed, crying about the sheer amount of everything happening ceaselessly. It must look self-destructive to observe me — an impulsive, self-loathing abuse survivor with PTSD — to allow the one solid and reliable aspect of my life, my marriage, to change fundamentally. It felt mutually self-destructive as my husband encouraged me to see other people.

It felt mutually self-destructive until I started speaking to people I connected with, people who understood my desire for submission and pain and being controlled. It felt mutually self-destructive until pieces of my brain I didn't realize were askew shivered into place, completing a puzzle I thought I'd finished years ago. It felt mutually self-destructive until I looked at my husband, lying down next to me, and felt more in love with him than ever before. What looks like mutual self-destruction from an outside perspective has been one of the most affirming, healing, necessary decisions for my marriage and my identity.

I met my husband my freshman year of undergrad, only months after leaving a long, intense, abusive relationship. We started dating that Spring semester, and our relationship felt embarrassingly close to a modern-day fairytale, or at least a mid-2010s indie film. It wasn't love at first sight, but it *was* a life-long commitment from almost the first date. I told him about my past, and he loved me anyway. He told me about his, and I loved him all the same. We processed our demons together, supported each other, and made each other laugh in ways nobody else could.

We changed together, grew into our truest shapes together. The first fundamental shift in our relationship came when I came out to him as bisexual, and shortly after, he came out to me as asexual. And I was scared. Sex was the first need I had that I knew he could not fulfill in the way I needed, not really, which repulsed me about myself. Bisexuality itself felt like an inherent, biological, inescapable sense of sexual greed and hunger, evidence that I was born to take and take and take until the love I cherish is destroyed. My frustration with my lack of sex — let alone the kink I refused to believe I wanted — felt like more evidence that I was so much of what the media says about bisexuals, and so much of what my abuser always said about me specifically.

As documented by GLAAD's annual "Where We Are on TV" reports, bisexual representation in media is becoming more common, and certainly more positive. This wasn't the case when I was young and in love with most of my best friends regardless of their gender. Even in 2018, articles were being written about bisexual representation like Gillian Brown's "Four Terrible Bisexuality Tropes on TV, and Four Portrayals That Defy Them" for *The Body Is Not an Apology*. Brown details that bisexuals largely follow four tropes in media:

1. The Slutty Bi trope, in which a bisexual character — usually female — is depicted as sexually promiscuous, almost incidentally bisexual, and written to appeal to a cishet male audience,

2. The Evil Bi trope, in which a character — usually male — has sex with men and women for the sake of manipulation, meaning they might not even be genuinely attracted to multiple genders,

3. The Unnamed Bi trope, in which a character is clearly bisexual but never explicitly stated as such or depicted in relationships with people of different genders, and

4. The Straight-to-Gay trope, in which a character assumes they are straight only to fall in love with someone of the same gender and come out as gay, versus suggesting that the character's very real attraction to people of multiple genders could ever be bisexuality.

The closest representation I saw for myself was Inara Serra in Joss Whedon's *Firefly*. Firefly is a space western set in the distant, semi-dystopian future, where a ruling class hoards the universe's wealth and the settlers on outskirt plants do everything they can to survive. Inara is a member of the core cast, a beautiful, glamorous, highly-respected sex worker who is shown to have both male and female sexual clients. This information about Inara comes as a shocking reveal, something the rest of the main cast clearly sees as taboo. Even in this far future, it seems, bisexuality is still something to be discussed only behind closed doors. Looking back, I wish I hadn't felt so grateful for the "representation" I got from *Firefly*, when what I actually got was another lesson that the fundamental, inextricable parts of myself make me harmful and impossible to love. All things my abuser had told me, too.

I took my husband's coming out in stride, and I adjusted. Longing for physical intimacy was genuinely a small cost compared to what I gained being in such a loving, healthy relationship. We got married about a year after graduating college. He supported me as I took a job that required us to move; he supported me as I left that job to pursue full-time writing; and he supported me as I came out as agender. Accepting what I have always known about myself, that I am as much a girl as a square with rounded corners is a circle, allowed more pieces of the puzzle of myself to lock together, but the fit was, at first, uncomfortably tight. Now I wasn't just a lecherous, gluttonous woman. I was an unknowable beast in a woman's skin, a siren selkie trying in vain to defy its need to lure and consume.

And the tropes suggested as much. There is no list I can provide here, because the only representation of agender beings in the media is aliens who don't understand the human concept of gender. The point is clear.

It was a need I felt often, and my husband knew this. He knew it when I hugged a friend too long and too tightly, or when I looked into a friend's eyes too deeply and too earnestly, or when a friend made me laugh almost how he makes me laugh. We were still in college the first time he suggested we try to open our relationship on my behalf. I balked at him, unable to fathom myself as yet another layer of greedy anathema. He'd bring it up every couple of years, and each time, I'd scoff.

And then it was 2020. I watched as a global pandemic killed over a million people worldwide. I watched as my friends in Portland were teargassed for over 150 nights in a row protesting for the protection of Black lives. I watched as political turmoil boiled over and turned into a grease fire. For the first time in my life, I both felt confronted by mortality *and* had become mentally and emotionally well enough to want to live a happy life. I'd spent years in therapy untangling my trauma. I'd distanced myself from the people who made me feel wrong for being bisexual or trans, and I'd gotten closer with a beautiful group of queer friends.

But confronted with mortality, I could no longer deny that I wanted more. I was in love with my husband; I still had more love inside me I needed to give. I was fine with my husband's asexuality; I still needed physical intimacy. I was healing every day more and more from my trauma; I still craved being pushed around, robbed of agency, compelled to do things I wouldn't do if not for the whims of someone else.

Like being agender, being polyamorous has few instances of positive representation. Desiring kink suggested that I was damaged, self-destructive, seeking cheap thrills until I brought everyone down into depravity with me. Regardless of rallying for polyam rights, loving and supporting polyam friends, it seemed impossible for me to be anything other than a cheater and a homewrecker. I felt not just destructive, but also forced back into a gender I'd been forced into most of my life. It was 2020, and I was destroying my marriage, and I was going to destroy others' marriages, and I was a horrid dysphoric creature simply not meant for this world. I was something from another planet or another world or a distant future. I was stuck here, now, and I would die destroying everything I loved.

But then I started actually speaking to potential partners. Most of them had been involved in polyamory and kink for years. When I told them what I was looking for, they were, of course, unfazed. Because what I was looking for, and who I am, are normal. Despite the way people like me are depicted in the media, despite the way sex and love are discussed, people like me exist everywhere. And as I was appreciated for the aspects of me I had always hated and feared, as I was so easily accepted and embraced and even desired, I started to actually accept that maybe I was made to be here after all.

To be explicitly clear, I do not feel like my desire for an open relationship *nor* my desire for kink is due to my history of trauma. As trans journalist and sex worker Ana Valens writes in her essay "The Next Muzzle on Sexual Expression" from her newsletter, Not Safe For Who?, "Whether it's bondage, sadomasochism, macrophilia, feederism, oviposition, foot fetishism, vore, you name it: there is no explanation for why we desire the things that we do. The trauma theory model — i.e.: we gravitate toward kinks related to our traumas — is a weak-kneed defense that's got more in common with pathologizing sex than sexual liberation." My sense of kink does not come from my trauma; long before meeting my abuser, my sexual fantasies always revolved around, essentially, being a sub. The same can be said for my polyamory. For as long as I can remember, the line in my heart between friendship and romance is so thin it is often invisible.

And the line became even blurrier as I started actively engaging in kink. When a friend and sexual partner told me to thank them for an orgasm after teasing and denying me for days, I did. I told them how grateful I was to be touch starved for them specifically in a year that mandates distance, because I was so thrilled to want them as much as I do. But in the rush of endorphins, I also thanked them for the ways subbing for them made my brain feel more like one organ instead of disjointed debris rattling around in my head. I thanked them for how healing this had been for me, and how much I needed it, despite telling myself I didn't for so long. The endorphins faded, but the gratitude remains.

When my husband came out to me as asexual, he was worried we were too mismatched and that I would leave him. I could objectively understand where he was coming from, but leaving him seemed so ridiculous to me that I honestly struggled to take his worries as seriously as I should have. Now, lying down next to him as I finally understood who I was and what I needed, I *truly* understood. As those final puzzle pieces slipped into place, I cried and told him how terrified I was to be myself. And I cried more, but differently, as he told me that was never going to change how much he loved me. I thanked him, and I continue thanking him still.

Dom By Day, Sub By Night

by Gina Tonic

My work as a dominant is the definition of a side hustle. One month I'm receiving birthday cards filled with twenty-pound notes, the next I'm throwing shoes at a man who knocked on my front door. I see it the same as having a Depop account: Occasionally, I might get a bit of money, but I don't have the time or energy to commit to making more than the odd bit of cash here and there.

Sex work has always had this kind of undercurrent in my adult life, from selling knickers on Reddit at nineteen to now, DMing school teachers wanking instructions after they have put thirty quid in my bank account. I find it especially easy to dominate sexually, because behind closed doors, I like to be dominated sexually. It is infinitely easier to match up to a person's fantasy when you know exactly what they're getting out of said fantasy. The release of giving up control to someone else, the taboo of wanting to be treated like shit, the unparalleled catharsis of submissive headspace.

With this innate understanding of why being dominated feels so great, I can understand why previous partners and potential dates have been confused about why I refuse to do so on an intimate level. In fact, it's not just a refusal in my case, but an inability. Vividly, I remember climbing on top of one ex, wrapping my fingers around his throat and crying before I had even managed to squeeze. This particular partner identified as a switch and it often got heated between us that I refused to be anything other than submissive with him.

In the time since, my most long-lasting relationships have revolved around a submissive and dominant dynamic, in which they take charge in the bedroom and I am the one being pushed around. Alongside this, in a parallel timeline, my dominant self-outside the bedroom has grown more confident in her abilities. Online domination — especially financially — has been my bag for a while, and now the occasional meetup has appeared too. While the encounters don't exactly make me wet, the power trip I get from making an adult man kneel at my feet and get sprayed in my spit is undeniable.

The adage "it's the quiet ones you need to look out for" is tossed around often in regards to our sexual relationships. The implication being that the more shy a person is day to day, the wilder they are in the bedroom. If that's true or not is beyond me but, in my experience, I can at least confirm the reverse: it's the loud ones you don't need to worry about. It's the loud ones who want to be taken over and dominated. For those not in the know, this can seem silly, or at least it always did to my Tinder matches.

When you're a loud, over the top kind of lady online and offline, those with a submissive nature swarm to you. You're the brightest light bulb in the room and much like a moth, they'd give anything to be burned by you. When the conversation turned to sex — I would always push for it to turn to sex — I would be as blunt as possible about wanting to be dominated. The people on the other side of the screen would always seem shocked. Not because they are necessarily opposed to slapping me around the face, but because they're looking to get slapped back.

Confiding that I can do that, but only for cash, caused one of two reactions: An agreement that maybe there isn't enough sexual chemistry to pursue a hook up, which was fine but frustrating after days of imagined dates and incessant flirting. The other was more aggressive — how can you perform for payment but not for a loved one, I'd get asked. How can you enjoy the power trip with a stranger, but not somebody you know on a deeper level?

Looking back on these feelings of inadequacy fellow submissives instilled in me when I was still in the dating game fill me with regret. Not because I didn't dominate them, but because I didn't stand up for myself and the difference between my roles as a sex worker and as a sexual partner.

Just as James Gandolfini and Tim Curry were shy in their real life, but played it big for their largely different, but similarly domineering characters of Tony Soprano and Dr. Frank-N-Furter, I find acting as a dominatrix having a similar feeling as taking to the stage. I am not being myself when I am being a sexual dominant, and I get a thrill from performing this star role and performing it well. Yet, instead of applause, my affirmations come from Cash App and gift cards.

Playing with power dynamics in this manner undoubtedly gives me pleasure, but it is not the same release I get from being submissive or that I get to give to my submissives. Considering the question of why I find myself unable to apply this pleasure to my standing - or newly forming - relationships, I find the answer also relating to acting, and from having to break character.

When being dominant has to factor in other aspects of a person, other than the blank slate I get from a submissive stranger, my mask slips. Considering kissing the other party, or cuddling them while watching a film, or introducing them to my family, makes me itch.

Just as much as I am not my dominant character, I need my partner to not be a submissive one. As furious as I would be if my partner told me they only saw me as a sub, even outside our bedroom, I have to be honest in my struggle to differentiate those identities in somebody else.

I don't believe this to be a deep psychological flaw on my part, but a fact of life. Just as some people can't see past a partner being attracted to feet, furries or other fetishes, I cannot find the attraction of dating someone who wants me to stand on their fingers and spit in their face. It feels as natural to me as being solely attracted to people with brown eyes, or people who are taller than me, or those from the same working class background as myself.

As much as a great relationship is about finding a middle ground, it is just as important to not settle either. We need to stick it out until we receive what we actually need from a partner, even if it means being single for a while. Or in my case, being single for four years.

What I have learned is that if someone sees my unwillingness to be dominant with them as a deep seated emotional flaw, that is their problem. If they want to be angry about it, that is their problem. What I truly hope is that my mismatched online matches that never came to be because of my requirements find similarly suited partners that tick all their boxes, without having to spit or stand on anyone they don't want to.

Keeping sex work as just that — work — makes my life simpler and ultimately, more satisfying. By setting standards of what I need in my real life, my sex life and my work life, and keeping those things separate, I find fulfillment without compromise.

The Purity Ceremony

by Shayna Conde

Growing up, my family and I were active members of a Pentecostal and Evangelical church called "The Assemblies of God" and, honestly, I have mostly fond memories of my times there. Being a high achieving and quirky Black girl in a predominantly white and Asian school system meant that I was the outsider in most of the spaces I entered, except for church. Not only was the youth group super diverse, but I was encouraged to be as weird as I wanted to be...to a point. And the line in the sand was purity under the watchful eyes of white Jesus (or, as I now call him, Ashton Christ). But I was cool with white Jesus and He seemed cool with me. Plus, I figured hey I took sex-ed; I read Christian books about relationships; I watched porn for research and immediately prayed away the sin from my immortal soul; clearly, I know things now. It wasn't until I moved into my college dorm that I realized the extent of the nothing I knew about anything.

Example number one: Puberty. Bodily changes aren't something that are accurately explained in sex education in the United States. Edit: Sex isn't something that is accurately explained in sex education in the United States, but it was all I had because asking about what was happening to my body in church was a non-starter. Anything vaguely sexual was not explicitly said to be off limits, but we all knew so we kept our secrets to ourselves and concocted theories about what was happening to our bodies. We were obviously wrong about most of it, but it's better to be wrong than damned at 12.

But I needed answers. So one Sunday, two boys in my grade and I decided to skip Sunday School (dangerous, I know) and spilled the beans. We got our bagels and hot chocolate and snuck into the Kids Church utility closet, which was right next to the first grade Sunday School class. Chris, Jordan and I whispered a pledge that: 1) We would be completely honest in answering any questions about puberty; and 2) What we ask/say would never leave that puppet-filled closet. Well, it's been about 15 years so I think the statute of limitations is up. I asked them "What is a 'ball'?," "What does 'hard' mean?," "Why do you all smell so bad now?," and "How do urinals work?," and they...tried their best to answer me. In return, I was asked "How many holes do you have?," "Do you have pubes, too?," "Which hole do you poop from?," and "What is a 'period'?," and I, too, tried my best to answer them. The three of us went back and forth for about 40 minutes, then we got ready for second service after we heard people putting chairs away next door.

We were around 17 years old when that conversation happened, and I figured there was nothing else I needed to learn from that point on.

Then Penis Day happened.

Penis Day was technically every Tuesday in October, November, and early December of 2011 (which was my first semester of undergrad). During my first semester, I had a work-study job for the athletic department of my university. I was essentially a laundry-lady; I was paid below minimum wage to wake up early, go into the football player's locker room after their practice, shovel out their germ-ridden clothes, toss them in a giant washing machine, and watch TV in the meantime. It was disgusting but simple work and I needed money for a gross amount of Burnetts and candy. I had two supervisors, one was a normal guy and the other, I eventually realized, was a sociopath who almost definitely abused cocaine. Let's call him "Allen". Allen was usually supervising my shift, and he would force me to go into the locker room and get the dirty clothes while the football players were still changing. He said if I didn't do it, he would fire me. So, being the ever obedient Christian girl who was taught to never talk back to men, I believed I had to do it. And thus, Penis Day was founded.

There were so many penises. Arguably, too many penises, especially for my previously penis-devoid eyes. Different colors, sizes, girths, a few bent ones; my initial theory about a "standard penis" was officially ruined. With time, the shell-shock of Penis Day wore off, for me and for the football players). Eventually, some of the players became more cocky (hehe), some would approach me and start conversations, two even asked me out on dates. Their proximity gave me more things to discover (while simultaneously trying to remain as not creepy as possible) like pubes. I had no idea that there were so many types of pubes and that it could cover so much, or so little, of their bodies.

I had so many questions and discoveries each Penis Day, and my suitemates found my lack of knowledge equal parts endearing and entertaining. It didn't take long for me to realize that before I started to understand anyone else's anatomy, it was more important that I understand my own, but that was a problem in itself.

Though Jesus did tell a group of men that it's better to gouge their own eyes out than to look inappropriately at a woman, there is a pattern in Scripture of a woman's form being innately sinful. From the problematic retellings of Delilah and Bathsheba to the many mentions of "the adulteress" and lust constantly being personified as a woman; daring to learn more about my body, as a young Black woman, felt hedonistic and damnable. This does not even take into account the gross hyper-sexualization of Black girls from the moment they are born, and I didn't need to understand this phenomenon to internalize it.

It took years for me to summon the courage to pick up a mirror and even look at my own vagina, never-mind to touch it. Masturbation was a sin and the want to act on it was something we (the youth, specifically) were encouraged to vigorously pray away, daily. When I was 13, I participated in a purity ceremony. In this ceremony, several teens and myself pledged to remain "pure" before the Lord and to not let anyone "be with us" until we were married. That included ourselves.

I remember standing across from my mom during this ceremony, seeing her look so proud of me and thinking maybe this will save me.

What nobody, knew, at that time (including myself) was that I had been sexually assaulted one year earlier. I didn't have the language for what happened, but I knew I needed to be cleansed. He was in the 8th grade, I was in the 7th, and I thought he was my friend. I believed that him grabbing my butt in drama club and squeezing my boobs when I slept during breaks in dress rehearsals meant that he liked me. I never had a boy "like" me, so this was the best attention I ever had. So when he pulled me into the boys bathroom one day, pushed my back against the metal flusher of the furthest stall from the door and tried to unzip my pants, I still thought this was happening because he liked me.

I don't remember much about that moment, to be honest. I remember his thick black curly hair and how moisturized it looked; I remember the cold metal against my back; I remember this deep voice that started in my gut and spread through my body that just screamed FIGHT; and I remember running until I found a friend walking through the halls and demanding that we talk about InuYasha or Naruto until we were called back to the auditorium to finish blocking the final half of Fiddler on the Roof. "Assault," "harassment," "violation," "trauma": these were not words I associated with myself for years. But "shame." Shame was mine to hold.

In my church, girls and women are taught to be careful of how we dress, speak, act, and exist because we should not "lead our brothers to sin against the Lord." I believed my innate feminine sinfulness, coupled with the feeling of impurity of my Blackness, was the inescapable enemy to my salvation and my safety. I told two people about what happened. One was a mutual friend of mine and his; she said I clearly misunderstood what happened. The other was a loner girl who said she believed me, but maybe she was just happy to have some company. Regardless, I believed that if I was holier, then Mark wouldn't have touched me, and what could possibly be holier than a purity ceremony?

After the ceremony, I immediately began to gaslight my own trauma. My biased sexual education said that sex was penetrative, and so the sexual trauma I was experiencing was unfounded because I was never penetrated. This logic of a phantom trauma was all I needed to send me spiraling into a self-harming addiction with suicidal inclinations; and let me tell you, you better believe I tried to pray it away. Did it work? Absolutely not. But copious amounts of therapy did.

Learning I needed to heal from the thing that was supposed to save my soul was a hard pill to shallow. It took years to recognize the nearly inaudible ticking sound of my own self-destruction and to recognize that the only person who can save me is me. My constant confusion, self-doubt and ignorance were all curable but I had to put in the work. I identified those feelings, gave them a voice and a name and communed with them until I could safely let them go.

The Nuclear Option

by Meaghann Ande

Nine years ago, my husband called me. He was at the apartment of one of his close college friends. "So."

"So?" *Oh lord, here we go,* I thought. We had been married for a little more than a year at this point – I could hear the tone of intrepid glee in his voice.

"Mason needs a place to stay temporarily." *Crap, what the hell am I going to say when Andy asks…* "What do you think about him staying with us for a month? Two, max."

Do I have a choice in the matter? "I mean… I really don't know him. And how would he feel about living with a kid?" My eyes flicked up to the pretty little boy lining cars up on the floor. In my mind I tried to conjure a picture of this surly weirdo that could have been one of our groomsmen. Had he been willing.

"It's fine. He knows the deal."

"All right, I guess? Where are we going to put him?" We were only 24: what was I to expect when we were the only ones in a stable living situation?

"In the office. He doesn't need a lot of space." The glee became more pronounced.

"There's not a lot of space – and then there's that office." The room in question was about seven feet by nine feet. There was a reason that it was being used as an office in our tiny home.

"It'll be fine."

I sighed silently and then asked, "when is he moving in?"

***

Three months later, Andy was on his third consecutive twelve-hour workday at the campaign office. "I really need you to come home." I said, looking down at the pregnancy test.

"I can't right now. I'm in meetings until 4:30. Can it wait?"

I looked at the clock. 9:13. "I guess."

"I'll see you then," he said and hung up.

"Seven hours…"

Mason walked into the kitchen and looked at me. "Everything okay?" he asked gently. This kindness was a side of him that was mostly new to me.

"I don't know." I looked up at those big brown eyes that were surrounded by dark hair and a beard pointing in every direction.

"You want to tell me what's going on?"

"I can't. I need to tell him first."

"Okay." He got a glass of milk from a fresh gallon.

"Do you really have to open another gallon of milk when the one in the fridge isn't empty?"

"That is purely Andy's backwash."

I gagged mildly and followed him into the living room. Glancing around, I studied the small but open space.

"What's the matter?" He remained kind but was as direct as always.

I slumped down onto the arm of the couch, giving in because the nerves were making me feel sick. "I'm pregnant."

"Isn't that what you guys wanted?" He asked cautiously.

"Yeah. But we just had a conversation yesterday about giving up. Living life with just one kid. I mean, Michael is five and a half! He's just going to be too old to tolerate a sibling soon."

"Michael will be fine. And Andy is going to be *happy*."

"He's not going to be home until 4:30… I think I started the conversation about giving up yesterday because I suspected." I was studying his untied boot laces as I said this, but looked up at him to ask, "Help me stay distracted?"

He studied my face for a moment, before saying, "I think I need colored lightbulbs for my room, so I don't have to use white light. It's so irritating! I'm thinking red and green."

"Where would you even find that?"

"I don't know. I'll figure it out." He said this as the knots in my stomach started to loosen.

When Andy got home that afternoon, I met him in the yard. "Are you pregnant?" He asked as he got out of the car.

I held up the pregnancy test. **YES**, it said, clear as day.

He shouted and grabbed me. "I knew it!"

I wrapped my legs around his waist so he could swing me around. "It's okay?" I asked in his ear.

"It's amazing."

That weekend, Mason accompanied our little family to a picnic across town. The democrats were having a party for one thing or another. I sat on a picnic bench across from him. "So."

"So?"

"Do you want to stay with us permanently?"

"Are you sure?"

"Yes."

He blew out a big breath. "Then yes."

***

It was the summer of 2014, and Andy had been working 70 hours a week, trying to get a good man elected to congress. While this would ultimately prove to be fruitless, he was killing himself to make it happen. Meanwhile I was at home with an autistic third grader and a busy toddler, while working full time.

Through all of this, Mason had my back – picking up a crying baby and distracting a bored seven-year-old when I was exhausted. He kept me occupied in the evenings, watching dumb tv shows, arguing over the ridiculous, and attempting to play board games that I had never heard of. We laughed, I cried, and the summer passed at a nauseatingly slow pace.

That August, Brooks was eighteen months old, and I was eighteen months into being completely overwhelmed by him. I did not realize yet that I was neck deep in the mire of post-partum depression. Andy was two counties over, on a multi-day excursion for the congressional campaign he was running.

Mason was pacing the living room, twirling his beard with his fingertips. He looked positively maniacal. "Would you please tie your shoes? You're going to fall down," I begged for the third time that morning alone.

"It's fine," he said, without so much as glancing down.

"I am absolutely not going to help you up when you finally fall on your face."

"I haven't yet."

I sighed. His pacing picked up speed. Any faster and he would be jogging. "If you keep clomping this path in my old house, you're going to fall through the floor."

"Newtown is terrible. Connecticut is terrible. It's shitty people surrounding a series of strip malls. It's ugly and grey."

"They're your parents and it's only ten days."

"It's going to be completely absent of absurdity." His packed suitcase was by the front door.

"We need to leave soon."

"Let's just go. If I wait any longer, I'm just going to get angrier."

"All right," I said and picked up the now shouting toddler. I did not say, "I'm going to miss you." He would not have had the first clue how to respond.

During his absence, we messaged on Facebook daily. I shared the ongoing shenanigans of our kids, and he kept me posted on the goings on in his corner of the northeast. I had heard at least monthly how completely he despised his hometown, and he made it clear that nothing had changed on that front.

"My sister is being awful – last night she stormed into my parents' room while they were sleeping and screamed at my mom."

"About what?!" Even then, I adored his mother. With her teaching career and crafting and constant nagging, she was the kind of mom I had always wished for. When his sister went off like this, I wanted to shout at her that she did not know what it was to have a difficult mother. My own being at a cross-section of bipolar and borderline personality disorders had made her difficult and abusive.

Andy and I were sitting on the couch watching *Diners, Drive-ins, and Dives* on one of his rare evenings at home. He looked over my shoulder at the screen of my laptop, "who are you talking to?"

"Mason. His sister is being a bitch again, so he's complaining to me rather than his mom."

"That's funny, I haven't heard from him at all since he left." Andy harrumphed and looked back to the TV.

"Huh, I've talked to him every day." I muttered as I typed. "This thing with Bea has him irate."

"She usually does," Andy said and glanced over at me while I continued to study my laptop screen.

Another message popped up, "You're keeping me from throttling her." I was so sad and angry for he and his mom.

"That's bullshit!" I shouted. "The need for musicians and story tellers has not somehow abated in the last five hundred years!"

"There may very well still be troubadours," he replied loudly, referring to my previous statement about George Strait, "but there are not traveling bards."

This was minute 48 of this argument.

Three nights later, I send him a video of a Peter Mulvey show at a small theatre in Portland. My message read, "Traveling. Bard."

"It's really not like having his best friend around. It's more like having 1.5 husbands and 2.5 children." I said for maybe the thousandth time in the six years he had been living within arm's reach. "There's no romantic relationship of anything, but I take care of him and he helps with the kids. He does have a really great smile though."

"I really don't understand the conversations you two have."

"Yeah. I know," I replied.

A year later he walked into my bedroom and handed me a knit turtle. "One of my mom's projects." He laughed, "since the turtle is your spirit animal."

This had come to light while Brooks and I were taking an online quiz a few nights before. Brooks's spirit animal, unsurprisingly, was a hummingbird.

"Something to keep watch when I'm gone." The year his parents had given him to finally get his shit together was nearly up. My heart started to pound, and my throat tightened. I looked up at him when the first tear fell. "It's going to be okay," he said and gently punched me on the shoulder.

I hung my head, unconvinced.

Over the next few days, I touched the small turtle on my dresser any time I walked by it. "It's going to be okay," I would whisper to myself.

A week later, Andy and I were having our twentieth tense conversation about the topic of Mason leaving while we were out one evening. "I'm just so tired of trying to help him. It never gets anywhere." He said tightly, "this is going to be good for him."

Another panic attack began to tighten my chest. "I really can't talk about this anymore." I said, and once again tears slid down my face.

"Fine." He replied and took a drink of his gin and tonic.

After we had left the restaurant, we ran to our favorite liquor store. Strolling through the parking lot, I joked to Andy, "I know the only things I could do to get you to leave me would be to sleep with Mason or vote for Trump."

"I don't care who you vote for," he feigned shock, "but you haven't slept with Mason?!"

"I know – weird, right?" I asked lightly. His hand tightened on mine and he frowned, so I said, "I've only been with one man since the summer of 2008." He pulled me closer and leaned his head on my shoulder when we stepped through the door of the store.

The next night, Mason and I were once again shouting at each other. This time, it was about the "OK Boomer" language that was circulating around the internet. Despite both being millennials, we had distinct and opposing views on this.

"I was raised by old people! It's disrespectful, trite, and dismissive!" I shouted at him.

"Which is exactly how they have treated us for the last fifteen years! After systematically decimating the economy and obliterating social security." Mason bellowed back at me.

"How does insulting an entire chunk of the population improve anything?" Everyone in the room was looking at us like we were insane. He watched me for a moment, and then strode out, slamming the door behind him.

Twenty minutes later, I was hanging out with one of our kids when my phone buzzed. I picked it up and began cackling at the meme that appeared on my screen. The image was of a small sailboat at sea, with the phrase "OK Schooner" over it in bold white letters. A second message popped up, "Yes, I did just waste a full ninety seconds looking for the right schooner picture."

I giggled so hard I had to lay my head down for a moment. "It's okay, I just spent a full two minutes laughing at that."

"Then it was worth it." This was his way of apologizing for yelling at me.

I chuckled and padded into the kitchen to make some tea. While waiting for the kettle to warm the water, I stood staring blindly at the counter replaying the scene in my head. I thought about how hard this person could make me laugh, and how frequently we spoke when he was not at home. I pondered the immense grief I felt every time I considered what my world would be like without him.

A fire bloomed in my chest and a cold sweat broke over my skin as this life-changing epiphany dawned on me. "Oh shit – I'm in love with him." I whispered to myself. The water in the kettle began to bubble while this feeling that I had been ignoring for years coursed through my veins. "How long…?"

As if it had been waiting for me to open the door, my mind offered up the answer to the question, sliding back to that summer of 2014.

Back in the kitchen on that chilly December evening, it occurred to me that Mason had quietly and systematically become one of my own best friends as well.

Two nights after that, I was in a terrible mood because Andy and I had been tense and argumentative for days. There did not seem to be even one area of agreement between us lately – especially when I had the courage to be honest with him about how I was feeling.

Mason walked in the back door while I was making dinner, chattering in his jocular tone. Hi voice and that tone were as familiar to me as any in my family, but the words were not connecting. He paused when he saw my face. "What's the matter?"

"I don't want to talk about it, but can I have a hug?"

"Of course."

For the first time in all the years I had known him, I wrapped my arms around his waist and laid my head on his shoulder. Up until this point, I had bro-hugged him. A quick arm around the shoulder and three thumps on the back. This was different. This was the kind of hug reserved for people that we are emotionally intimate with.

I inhaled deeply through my nose, truly absorbing the scent of him for the first time. Fire burned through my muscles and bones, as if carried in on the air that moved in my lungs. I stepped back in shock, turning away quickly lest he see it on my face.

"Meg."

"Yeah?"

"What's wrong?"

"Andy just doesn't get that he's blowing me off to work again! As if the fact that it's only Lyft makes up for the fact that he's never here!" I punted to the underlying issue modulating my mood. It was so much safer than telling him the rest.

"He's just trying to make money."

"Just like always. Please don't excuse his behavior right now."

Mason held up his hands in silent acquiescence.

"I want my husband more than I want the money! I want to be his priority just once!" This stream of consciousness ranting continued while I made pasta for us. "He never just stops to listen to me. And if I do manage to get his attention, he interrupts before I get a full sentence out."

"That's how he is, Meg. He interrupts everybody."

"I know..." I sighed, running out of steam. "Want to watch some Brooklyn Nine-Nine while we eat?"

"Yeah." He said it kindly. I could see that he was planning to stick with me on this night. I could see that he was concerned about my state of mind. It occurred to me that he may well know me better than anyone else did.

I crashed into the wingback recliner in the office, and he settled into the swivel chair. Studying this man who was eternally at my side, I decided to tell him everything. "Recently in therapy I realized that I have severe PTSD and that it's been causing me to dissociate for three years or more. I haven't felt hardly anything. And Andy won't listen. He ignores or interrupts me when I try to tell him how much this has impacted our life together. I swear to god, he thinks we're happy!"

Mason set down his bowl and then took mine to do the same. He wrapped his hands around mine, and watched me while I continued to rail about my childhood, the pain and fear, how much I *did not* remember, and why my mind had chosen to disconnect from it. I relayed how much it hurt when Andy would tell me I needed space and walk away without listening.

Tears ran down my face in the same uninterrupted stream as the words that were tumbling out of my mouth.

"I knew you were struggling, but I didn't know things were this bad."

"How could you when I've gotten so good at hiding it?" My head fell even further as the tears briefly became sobs.

He waited it out, watching me steadily.

I could not help myself, so I finished with, "And to top it all off, I realized a couple nights ago that I have feelings for someone else. Someone who does listen. Someone who is always there. Someone I trust implicitly. And I don't know what to do."

He paused, knowing me well enough to understand what I was telling him, and well enough not to run with it. "Well, would you do anything about it if you could?"

"No? I don't know. I don't think so?" I paused before the whole story fell out of my mouth. "I don't want to blow up my life."

"Then there's your answer."

How Casual Sex Turned Into A Toxic Relationship With A White Supremacist

by E. Jamar

Growing up as a disabled woman in the United States, I was never viewed as a sexual being. Disabled people are often infantilized to the point of assumed asexuality. It wasn't until I moved out on my own at age twenty that I had the opportunity to explore my sexuality, gender, and relationships. I had no idea what my stances were on much of anything, but I knew I wanted to have sex, and at my core I just wanted to be loved. No one taught me much about sex, though, and no one ever taught me about self-respect. So I had to teach myself.

Unfortunately, I am the master of crash-coursing my way through most things in life; dating and sex wouldn't be any different. My relationship to sex when I first lived on my own was unhealthy at best. At age twenty-three, I lost my virginity on a one night stand to a man I met online who I would never see again. And from the moderate to severe porn addiction that I developed over the years, to the internalized ableism that left me believing that I wasn't worthy of being viewed as a sexual being in the first place, it was only a matter of time before I found myself in a toxic situation. The same year, I met a different man on Tinder, he was a white supremacist.

I created dating profiles and put myself out there without a clue about what I was doing. To my surprise, dozens of men wanted to have sex with me. After a few less-than-satisfying sexual partners, and a summer-fling with a narcissist who didn't understand the word "no," I was reaching the end of my rope in terms of men. Still reeling from the violations from the last fling, I coped by trying to find another warm body to distract me. Attention from men was still a coping mechanism of mine, so I downloaded Tinder. I promised myself that I would at least raise my standards this time, so fuckboys were out of the question. While most people who messaged me only said "hi", one guy named "Kyle" asked me an intriguing question about my career.

Kyle was an engineering student at a school just a mile away from me, and he was cute — in an awkward kind of way. I thought, "He'll do." Engineers are certainly not my type since the running joke is that they're practical and emotionless to a fault. Being a creative professional who embodies toxic empathy, you could say that we were polar opposites. While a far cry from an ideal match, he seemed interesting enough, and if anything, he was interested in me.

The first red flag I overlooked was his comment on a photo of me wearing a "Black Lives Matter" t-shirt. He asked sarcastically if I was okay with seeing a "white devil," then he complimented me on my appearance. It was this push and pull game that reeled me in from the beginning. Right away he knew how to push my buttons, and I took the bait every time. I challenged him every step of the way, arguing my points and teasing him right back. I was never one to give in, and he liked the fight. I'd criticize his libertarianism and in the same breath joke, "I don't know if I can have sex with you, being the white devil and all." This sick version of having a distaste for each other's political views and social stances, our warped form of flirting, was just a precursor to how twisted this relationship would become. After a few days of incessant text exchanges, we decided to meet up for dinner.

The date was as awkward as you can imagine. After an hour of half-hearted conversation, I pulled out from our table and told him I was going home. I let him know that I lived within walking-distance, and he insisted on walking me home. This confused me since the date was so bad. I told him "No" three different times, but he insisted. He didn't respect my wishes, and I should have taken this as a red flag.

We walked the four blocks to my apartment, and talked along the way. Since a friend was at my place anyhow, I offered for him to come in for a moment. We had painfully awkward small talk before he finally left. Later that night, he texted me about how great of a time he had. I was flabbergasted and replied, "I couldn't tell." He said, "I couldn't read you since your body language is so subtle, but I wanted to touch your leg." To this day I'm still not sure why I flirted back, but it was obvious that this relationship was purely sexual.

A few days later, he kissed me just to "get it out of the way." It was the quickest, most emotionless kiss I had ever experienced. This was also the first time he picked me up out of my wheelchair, and I was pleasantly surprised by how willing he was to handle me. Most men are worried and need a lot of guidance, but he jumped right in. Despite every cringe-worthy moment, I liked that he didn't care that I was disabled.

Our first time having sex was no different. We were finally alone in my apartment, and after some cuddling, our clothes came off. With a deadpan look on his face, he said, "What if I told you right now that this was my first time?" I gave him a look, and he started laughing and told me he was kidding before quickly going down on me. I've felt confused with every man I've had sex with, but this was different. He was still awkward, but this time it wasn't because of my disability. It was something else. We barely kissed, and no matter how ravenous I was, I couldn't feel any passion from him. On one hand, I liked that I could tell him what to do and it didn't phase him; he wasn't nervous to move my body in the slightest. I found his body attractive and I felt confident in my own body when I had sex with him. But on the other hand, I had to turn my mind off to get any real pleasure out of it. He came instantly; I didn't.

The thing I liked most about our situation was that I could be brutally honest. At this point, we made it clear that we were friends with benefits, so there was no holding back. I told him how bad the sex was, and his insecurities came seeping out. He needed to keep trying to prove that he had done his homework, and so we tried for months. Some nights were better than others, but still largely unmemorable. It was clear: he wanted someone to practice sex with, and I wanted to feel attractive. It was a mutual agreement.

However, as the months went on, the "friends" part of "friends with benefits" came to the forefront. He confided in me about his insecurities and his upbringing. He told me about his narcissistic mother and his bad luck with women, and I started to feel bad for him. Each day it was a new story about how the world just didn't understand his intentions. Whether it be someone he slept with calling him racist, or not wanting to be touched by him entirely, he always had a drawn-out explanation about why they were mistaken. It may seem obvious now, but it wouldn't be until much later when I'd put the pieces together and learn that this sympathy-seeking stemmed from something much more sinister.

After countless hours of hearing his seemingly vulnerable confessions, my heart for him was softening. The manipulation was working. I always empathized with his struggle and he played on that — not to mention that he was damn convincing. At this point, we started going on dates regularly. He met some of my friends and began spending the night. The line between casual sex and casual dating was rapidly blurring.

I started becoming frustrated that we weren't actually dating, because deep down I knew I deserved it. I knew I was worthy of commitment, and I was selling myself short. It's one thing to casually sleep with someone, but the level of emotional labor I was putting into this man was something else entirely. I still felt confused, but I asked him to meet me for coffee and put my cards on the table. I told him I'd developed feelings, and that I thought we should give it a try. He went into a long monologue about how dating me was just "ineffable." I didn't fight him on it, I had more self-respect than that.

After coffee, he walked me back to my apartment. He had class soon and had to leave, but he wouldn't stop staring into my eyes. He sighed and said, "You know, I really need to leave if I'm going to make it, but all I want to do is get naked with you." I teased him, "is that so?" Suddenly, he was kissing me, and for the first time ever, I could feel his intensity. I was weak in the knees and gave in immediately. We tore each others' clothes off — never getting close enough, never quick enough. It was like all of the arguments, and tension, and disagreements were built up to this moment, and it was the hottest, dirtiest sex we ever had. When we laid next to each other afterward, we both talked about how nice it was to cuddle, and I couldn't help but think that this felt like a relationship.

I didn't see him for two weeks after that night, and decidedly moved on. That's when he texted me. He said he wanted to date me "for real" because he realized how I made him feel. I was furious, forced him to say it to my face, and chewed him out. We left that conversation as a couple.

I had my doubts from the beginning, but I liked having someone by my side. I felt vindicated that someone finally wanted to commit to me, and I saw the good in him even if it was all a show. He fed me lies but tied them up as pretty promises in shiny bows, with no follow-through. He was a sorry excuse for a partner. I fell head over heels for someone who only gave me scraps of true affection. I regret a lot of things, but I don't regret loving a flawed human. I do regret loving someone so flawed as to devalue human life, including my own.

To no one's surprise, our fights began immediately. They were gut-wrenching and never-ending. We went back and forth for hours on end because he could never stop, pushing me relentlessly in an effort to get me to cave in. We fought because he was rude to all of my friends and made them uncomfortable. We fought about his ableism, racism, and how his privilege played a role in our relationship (and the world.) This happened weekly, and only escalated as time went on. He got angry and sobbed because he couldn't understand how he had any privilege. Because of my physical disability, he knew I couldn't get away during our fights, so he would trap me, get in my face, scream, and rip his hair out if I told him he was wrong. While I was bawling, hyperventilating, begging him to take a break, he blamed me. He claimed my PTSD was the source for all of our problems, but this had nothing to do with my mental health. It was emotional abuse.

Soon enough we were living together, because he was broke. Money was a huge point of contention in our relationship. I paid for everything. Not only did he control me financially, but he increasingly convinced me to let him help me with my personal care instead of my paid assistants. I was trapped, but I coped. It wasn't until the night of the Wisconsin governor's election that I knew I needed to leave. After many budget cuts under Walker, disabled people needed a democratic win to survive. Kyle knew this intimately.

Up until this point, our opposing political views were never tangible, but that night he admitted he voted third party. At first, the conversation was casual. I tried to understand his point of view, but it quickly became offensive. He started spewing ableist rhetoric, right-wing propaganda, and racist remarks about our city. My mind went blank. I told him, "I don't think I can be with someone who won't help fight for my rights." He was livid, and we fought the entire night. He admitted that he didn't agree with any equality movements, especially in regard to racism, but kept quiet because I would argue. It was horrifying. The only thing I remember vividly was him screaming in my face about how unfair I was being. About how he didn't have privilege. About how equality already existed. He had a habit of digging his nails into his arms, and all I could see was blood dripping down his forearms as desperate tears rolled down his face. I'll never forget that image.

I didn't leave for nearly two years. I tried a handful of times. Our lives were completely intertwined, and I was scared about what he would do if I left. I knew about his only two other serious relationships before me and how with the first, he faked a suicide attempt to manipulate her, and the other, he hired a "dating coach" to listen in on their private calls and to try and get her back. At this point, I didn't know what he was capable of, but I knew in my heart that he was a white supremacist. For self-preservation alone, I held out as long as I could. No matter how many times I look back and think of what I could have done, I know I couldn't have left any sooner — not with a master manipulator whispering in my ear every step of the way.

After he came home from a long work trip where he cheated on me, we fought for eight hours straight. I broke up with him several times and he begged for me to stay over and over. He knew my insecurities and he played on them. He tried using sex as an incentive, because he knew that sex was what pulled me in from the start. He told me he would be more affectionate, because all I wanted was love. He almost convinced me, until after eight hours of fighting he told me again that I was unreasonable, and it finally hit me: I was being used. I forced him to put me in my wheelchair and said, "You took advantage of me. Get out." He tried to hug me, he tried to sweet talk his way through it. I didn't budge. He spent the night in a hotel, and I had all of his things packed up that same night. It was the bravest thing I've ever done.

After the breakup, everything became terrifyingly clear. I didn't *just* break up with someone who was obviously a narcissist, possibly a sociopath, and abusive, but also someone who eerily aligned with white supremacy. Little twisted stories he told came rushing back to my mind. He admitted all of it to me, I just couldn't let myself hear him.

From admitting that his monologues were from TV shows, to studying attraction theory in depth to trick women, it was obvious that he was misogynistic, but this insecurity ran deeper. Not only did he follow Jordan Peterson as one of his disciples despite his racism, he wanted to be him. He refused to denounce Donald Trump on any level, and it was becoming clear he followed him. I finally remembered every time he talked about his ex-girlfriend and how he was disgusted because she loved her Hispanic heritage. I remembered how after every fight he told me that I should *"Go date a black man"* if I disagreed with him. More and more red flags came rushing back into my mind, and upon hearing about the breakup, my closest friends admitted that they were always afraid for me.

I mistook sexual intimacy for real intimacy because I wanted to believe it; I wanted to believe him. I fell in love by mistake and couldn't get out until it was too late. I ignored so many red flags that I couldn't see what was right in front of me — a truly dangerous person. He saw the good in me and thought he could profit off of it, and in many ways did. He hid his prejudices behind his progressive, queer, disabled partner. It was the perfect ploy.

Truth be told, I don't know much about being a white supremacist, or joining the alt-right movement, but I know what it was like to date Kyle. His white supremacy may be insidious, but it makes it all the more dangerous. I know in my gut that he dehumanized marginalized people in words and in action, and that Fox News was his church. I know the fear that came with leaving him because it still keeps me up at night, and I would never be surprised if I were to see his face on the news for something unfathomable.

Ugly Couple
by CT Marie

At 22, I started working at a restaurant in the West Village. The restaurant was an old neighborhood joint, a place with no cameras or managers. That first week, I stuttered and stumbled through my shifts. In the kitchen, the chef would pass me plastic cups of gold tequila to cool my nerves. My coworkers were friendly, but they all despised Nate, the head bartender.

"Nate's behind bar tonight, so no drinking on the floor," My coworker, Jen said.

"Nate's a son of a bitch," My other coworker said.

"He's Mitchell's little spy," Jen added. Mitchell was the owner.

Nate was 49 with shaggy blonde hair and had a slight English accent. He wore floral button downs and slip-on checkered vans. He drank rosé and smoked Winstons. He was newly married, to a woman 15 years his junior, who my coworkers felt sorry for, because, according to them, Nate was a piece of shit.

That night, after Mitchell left, I drank several shots of tequila in the kitchen. Walking into the dining room, I saw that Nate's back was turned to me. I took the opportunity to pour myself a drink. Just as I reached for the tequila bottle, Nate turned around.

"What are you doing?" He snatched the bottle out of my hand.

"Making a drink."

"For who?" His pale blue eyes scanned the dining room.

I couldn't help but laugh. In response, Nate grabbed my ear and twisted it. I was filled with a jolt of excitement that spread up to my face. He smelled of cigarettes and detergent.

"You stay on your side and I'll stay on mine." Nate hissed, letting go of my ear.

The next day, I found out Nate had tried to get me fired.

"Don't worry, we all stood up for you," Jen assured me.

I watched Nate flirt with female barflies and high five Mitchell, as he walked out the door. Whatever power Nate had in the restaurant I wanted it too. He was a challenge, something to conquer and then throw away. Nate and I kept our distance, for a month.

It was Christmas Eve. I had dressed up for the occasion, but felt unattractive. I was heartbroken over a guy who didn't feel the same way about me. Muttering profanities to myself, as I entered an order into the POS system, Nate, on his way to the bathroom, brushed past me and said, "You have a hole in your stocking."

While Nate was in the bathroom, I poured myself a glass of wine that I downed. I was closing that night and the tables had started to clear. There was barely anyone at the bar. At midnight, I sat at Nate's bar and willed him to give a shit. To my surprise, he poured me a glass of wine.

"Merry Christmas!" he said cheerfully.

"Merry Christmas," I said.

"Aren't your parents expecting you home?" He asked.

"They're asleep." I replied.

I don't remember what we talked about. All I know is, whatever thoughts unraveled out of my mouth Nate connected with. Perhaps, he hated himself too.

Around 2 AM, we were in the bathroom together where he offered me a bump of blow. I snorted the white powder between his thumb and forefinger, and impulsively asked, "Do you want to see my tits?" I pulled down the front of my dress.

We shared a passion for losing our minds on a nightly basis. Nate would brush his finger against the waistline of my jeans or under the bottom of my shirt. We would pass each other bags of blow under the service bar and in crumpled tissues. We would meet each other in the bathroom.

Nate and I consummated our relationship at my apartment. My parents were out of town. We awkwardly fumbled with each other's bodies like shy teenagers. Afterwards, Nate wouldn't look at me and got dressed quickly. In a hurry to get away, Nate barreled down the stairs of my building. It was a fuck and run, surreal and dirty. I took a shower and wiped myself clean.

Eventually, we got caught. The man who cleaned the restaurant overnight filmed me and Nate overstaying our welcome, and of Nate putting bottles of rosé into his man purse. Mitchell fired Nate and slut shamed me, saying my clothes were inappropriate, as if that was the reason.

Every time I went to work, I felt like I had a scarlet letter burned into my waiter apron. My coworkers gossiped, bar regulars talked, and the guys in the kitchen smirked. To my surprise, nobody alerted Nate's wife, so we continued to see each other.

Having sex with Nate was like being addicted to fast food. It warmed my face, made me sweat, and the satisfaction was immediate, but I was left feeling queasy. If we couldn't go to Nate's house or mine, we met in dimly lit cafes. We kissed on deserted side streets and dark corners of empty bars. We were an ugly looking couple, but I liked how he looked at me. I needed him to touch me. Otherwise, I felt nothing at all.

When his wife was out of town, Nate would invite me over. He lived in an East Village studio apartment, close to the park. Lying on his bed, I would shut my eyes and cover the top part of my face with a pillow. I wasn't self-conscious, but I was ashamed of my attraction to him. Nate enjoyed pleasing me. Getting me off got him off. He used his hands and mouth to press all my buttons. He would whisper that he loved me and I would slur it back.

The problem with these kinds of relationships is that they fool you. You're momentarily convinced the love is real, and then you wake up with a hangover. I didn't enjoy sleeping over at his place. In the morning I was just dirty sheets stripped off a bed.

On one occasion, Nate had something "special" to show me. On his wall was a large framed illustration of a 1950s pin-up girl.

"It makes me think of you," he said.

"You tell your wife the same thing?!" I said.

Turning away, he asked, "Do you want a drink?"

Do you want a drink? Do you want a smoke? Do you want some blow? Do you want to screw? We didn't ask each other too many other questions. Our conversations weren't deep. I was a cartoon to Nate, a fantasy. To me, he was a rebound, a distraction.

Nate started working at a bar that was a 15 minute walk from the restaurant. He worked till 4 AM on the nights I worked till 11 PM. I visited him often. Nate palmed me $60 and sent me on missions to score blow from his friend, who bartended at a dive around Canal Street. His friend handed me the blow in matchbooks. I would swig down a Pacifico and help myself to the contents of the matchbook in the bathroom, and then I would return to Nate's bar to deliver the prize.

Those nights sucked me dry. I would wake up half drunk, my nose caked with dry blood and white powder. I had no motivation to do anything but wait for my restaurant shift to start, so I could repeat myself.

Nate and I became predictable. When he came over to my place, his wife would call constantly. When he disappeared into the night, she would go looking for him. I didn't intend to steal Nate away. I knew our relationship had an expiration date. I wasn't in love.

Nate's wife became very sick. She was going in and out of the hospital, and he wouldn't tell me why. Eventually, she was taken in by her parents to be cared for.

"You can't take care of her?" I asked Nate.

"I have a daughter who needs caring," he said.

I shouldn't have been surprised that he only cared about his five year old. Apparently, she was the result of a one night stand with an Italian woman he couldn't stand, or so he said. His daughter covered the walls of his apartment and the only picture he had of his wife was stuck on the corner of the fridge.

At 25, I went cold on Nate. He smelled like a wine glass that needed to be washed. I was afraid I would start smelling the same. It was easy to turn my back on Nate. He was never emotionally there for me to begin with. I needed to better myself or I was going to die, or worse... End up like him.

Months later, I found out, through bar regulars, that Nate's wife had passed away. I didn't know she was that sick, but I knew she loved Nate and he drove her crazy. It wasn't entirely my fault, but I was an enthusiastic contributor to his bad behavior for three years. I was guilty to some extent.

Nate and I poisoned ourselves in the spirit of having fun without responsibility. Sometimes, I pass the window of his workplace. I can recognize that blonde head from anywhere. Now he is just a dark memory of a time when I was ugly.

About the Authors

Kyra Wolfe

Kyra Wolfe is a health and lifestyle journalist. Her main focus areas are sex, relationships and mental health.

Allyson Darling

Allyson is a wordsmith who creates collections of paragraphs about things that really happened. She especially likes writing about mental health, sexuality, and the nuances of being a human being.

Jenelle Parish

Jenelle Parrish is a writer and creative director based in New York, NY.

Jeana Jorgensen

Jeana Jorgensen is a scholar, dancer, and sex educator. Her work focuses on gender roles, culture & sexuality, and feminist issues, as well as folklore topics that intersect with gender and sex.

Molly Godfrey

Molly Godfrey is a writer and viral content creator and the 'go-to' relationship coach for high-achieving women in their 30s. She has been recognized as a trusted love advisor, helping her clients get unstuck and land their dream relationship. Her essay, "3 Mini Agreements to Make With Your Partner" was first published at *Medium/PS I Love*, Oct. 7, 2020.

Shane Thomas

Shane Thomas earned a Masters degree at the College of Arts and Sciences at USC, where he taught Freshman Writing for ten years. His work has appeared in *Reed Magazine, Sliver of Stone, The Tower Journal, Slow Trains, Alabama Literary Review, Adelaide, Crack the Spine, The Sand Hill Review, Existere, Forge, Hobo Pancakes, storySouth, the Penmen Review, Shark Reef, the T.J. Eckleburg Review,* and *The Sun Magazine.*

Almaz Ohene

Almaz Ohene (she/her) is a Freelance Journalist writing on representation, diversity, inclusion and sexuality – with an intersectional focus – for a range of leading publications, including *British Vogue, Campaign, Stylist* and *VICE*. She is the Founder of 'Kayleigh Daniels Dated', a web platform combining raunchy stories with informative health features to encourage and normalise free and frank discussion about sexuality. She is part of the Decolonising Contraception Collective – a community interest group working within sexual and reproductive health – and is also a Sexual Health Education Facilitator with the School of Sexuality Education (formerly Sexplain), an independent organisation running inclusive and comprehensive sex ed workshops in schools. Almaz is also a classically trained violinist and has appeared on stage, national television and at music festivals with several London collectives.

Melissa Gabso

Melissa Gabso (she/her) is a writer, graphic designer, and illustrator living in central Connecticut with her husband and two four-legged house gremlins. She writes science fiction and personal narrative, creates branding and publications for a number of nonprofits, and draws realistic landscapes and portraits with colored pencil. Her most recent artwork can be found on Instagram @melnessguru.

Catherine Renton

Catherine Renton is a UK-based writer specializing in mental health, sex, sobriety and culture who has written for *Vogue, Elle, Cosmopolitan, Refinery29, NBC News, and NY Mag* among others. She can be found tweeting @rentswrites.

Douglas Moser

Douglas Moser is a theatre director with over 30 years of experience, regionally and in New York. He made his opera debut directing the premiere of "Patience & Sarah," the first groundbreaking lesbian opera, at Lincoln Center. Winner of the Connecticut Critics' Award for his "A Christmas Carol" at the Westport Country Playhouse. He directed the world premiere of Glacier Bay, starring Jack Klugman and Brett Somers screen adaptation starring James Noble and Dorothy Bryce won numerous awards on the festival circuit. Douglas developed work at the O'Neill Theatre Center, NY Theatre Workshop, UM Theatre Festival, and American Opera Projects.

His production of "Spinning" premiered at the Long Wharf, where he workshopped his "Elegy for Ebenezer." Memoir pieces have been published in *Echo, Peculiar, Paragon Press, and The Good Men Project*. Currently completing a comic thriller, James and Jim, developed at the Writers Hotel, and Pussy Boy, developed at the Yale Writers' Conference.

Becca Beberaggi

Becca Beberaggi is a Los Angeles based writer, visual artist, and singer (under her musical persona Roselina Albino) born and raised in New York City. She has studied at The Art Students League of New York, Stella Adler Studio of Acting, T. Schreiber Studio Of Acting, HB Studios, Upright Citizens Brigade, and The Labyrinth Theatre Company. Previously serving as the comedy producer at Paste Magazine, Becca has also had some of her writing featured in magazines like *Eloquent Mag, Paste*, and *oc87recoverydiariesshe*, commonly writing about comedy, diversity, and mental health.

Stephanie Parent

Stephanie Parent is a graduate of the Master of Professional Writing program at the University of Southern California. After working for six years at a commercial dungeon in Los Angeles, three as a submissive and three as a switch, performing both dominant and submissive sessions, she's now writing about her personal and professional experiences with BDSM. Stephanie is also a published author of poetry and fiction, and her poetry has been nominated for the Rhysling Award and Best of the Net.

Hattie Gladwell

Hattie Gladwell is a freelance writer specialising in mental health, women's health, sex, relationships, parenting and pregnancy. She has bylines in *Metro, Cosmopolitan, Marie Claire, Prima, SheKnows, Grazia, The Independent, The Daily Mirror, HuffPost, The Telegraph, Greatist, Healthline, Yahoo! Style, Tyla, LadBible, Happiful* and more.

Blake Turck

Blake Turck is a freelance writer, storyteller and native New Yorker. She has had bylines in *She Knows, MotherFigure,* and *Huffpost* (which listed her personal essay as one of the best of 2019).

Joe Duncan

Joe Duncan is a writer and political activist from Los Angeles, California. His essay, "The Joys of Dating an Older Woman" was first published at *Medium,* Aug 30, 2019.

Elena Fernández Collins

Elena Fernández Collins is a writer and a podcast critic and podcaster for places like *The AV Club, Bello Collective*, and *Podcast Review.* For her essay, "Why Have I Only Dated White People?," she wishes to give special thanks to Erin Kyan and Wil Williams.

Lisa Levy

Lisa Levy is a writer, essayist, and critic. Her work has appeared in many publications, including *the New Republic, the LARB, the Believer, the Millions, the Rumpus, TLS, the CBC,* and *Lit Hub*, where she is a contributing editor. She is also a columnist and contributing editor to *Crime Reads.* She is currenntly pursuing an MFA in nonfiction writing at Goucher College. Her essay, "Weight and Dates" was first published at *Medium*, February 26, 2020.

Marcus K. Dowling

Marcus K. Dowling is a Washington, DC resident and full-time freelance journalist. In the sex/kink space, he writes for *Kinkly, Future of Sex*, and *HotMovies*. In the non-sexual space, he has bylines for the *Bitter Southerner, VIBE, Complex, VICE, The FADER, Bandcamp, GRAMMY, LEVEL, Mixmag*, and more.

D. Anne Tolentino

D. Anne Tolentino is a writer and journalists with bylines at *Vulture Bustle, Instyle, Studyhallxyz*, and more.

Alexandra Hogan

Allie Hogan is a Brooklyn-based writer who is passionate about covering sex, relationships, and mental health. She is an assistant editor at *Best Life* and a staff writer for *The Rational*, where she produces the 'Laid Bare' column, a series that explores the intersection of sex and mental health. She co-hosts *The Rational's* 'What You Came For' podcast, where she interviews a variety of experts about the culture of sex and takes a deep dive into distinct subtopics. She is currently working on her debut novel.

Danielle Chelosky

Danielle Chelosky is a New York-based writer who specializes in essays about love and sex.

Vonnnie Wright

Vonnie Wright is a Major in the United States Army and a writer.

Jennifer Greenberg

Jennifer Greenberg is a Montreal-born writer and editor based in New York. Formerly an editor for *Time Out Israel* and *Atmosphere Magazine*, she has written for such publications as *The Forward*, *The Jerusalem Post*, and *The Canadian Jewish News*.

Suzannah Weiss

Suzannah Weiss is a writer who has written about feminism, sex, and other fun topics for *The New York Times*, *The Washington Post*, *New York Magazine*, *Vice*, *Glamour*, *Playboy*, and many other publications. She has served as an editor for *Teen Vogue*, *Vice*, and *Complex*, and discussed gender and sexuality on many radio shows, podcasts, and conferences including SXSW. Her essays have been published in several books, and Whoopi Goldberg once cited one of her articles on "The View" in a debate over whether asking for what you want in bed is a feminist act. (Suzannah would say it is.)

Carolyn Busa

Carolyn Busa is a writer/comedian living in Brooklyn, NY. She's written for *Greatist*, *Allbodies*, *HelloGiggles* and maintains the blog *My Sex Project*. Carolyn has also written stories for Eforia, the sexual discovery and wellness app.

June "Moon" Sadler

June Sadler is a storyteller, utilizing all media to deliver a pop culture laced oral herstory. Her writing is a prayer, a rhythmic verse bundled in melodies wandering the musical galaxies between soul and hip hop.

Rachael Davies

Rachel Davies is a freelance journalist and copywriter from Edinburgh, Scotland.

Mike McClelland

Like Sharon Stone and the zipper, Mike McClelland is originally from Meadville, Pennsylvania. He has lived on five different continents but now resides in Georgia with his husband, their two sons, and a menagerie of rescue dogs. He is the author of the short fiction collection *Gay Zoo Day* and his creative work has appeared or is forthcoming in *The New York Times*, *Boston Review*, *Vox*, *The Baffler*, and a number of literary magazines and anthologies. He's a graduate of Allegheny College, The London School of Economics, and the MFA program at Georgia College, and is currently a PhD candidate in the University of Georgia's Creative Writing program.

Aitza Burgess

Aitza Burgess is a Black American writer based in Spain. She creates content at the intersection of feminism, pop culture, and Black womanhood.

Stephanie Conway

Stephanie Conway is a freelance writer originally from Northern England, who moved to LA at 18 on her own. After first spending a decade working on celebrity PR campaigns and brand marketing strategy at a global agency, she escaped reality to live and work as a digital nomad on the tropical paradise island of Lombok in Indonesia.

Wil Williams

Wil Williams (they/them) is a journalist and podcaster based in Phoenix, Arizona. They are the CEO of Hug House Productions, a podcast production and consultation agency, and the showrunner of VALENCE, a serialized urban fantasy fiction podcast about a queer found family rebelling against data mining and unethical experimentation. For their essay, "No Longer Terrified to Be Myself," they wish to give special thanks to Elena Fernández Collins.

Gina Tonic

Gina Tonic is a creative freelance culture journalist based in Manchester, but originally from the Valleys in South Wales. Originally Gina Jones, she decided to update her name to match her favourite bev and all her bylines can be found under the moniker Gina Tonic. She champions a feminist perspective in her work, and as well as writing, she has been a collaborator and editor at *Polyester Zine*. Her work as an editor and curator has led to the creation of her own publication *The Fat Zine*, co-founded with photographer Chloe Sheppard. She also works as the sex and relationships editor for *The Breakdown*.

Shayna Conde (she/her)

Shayna Conde (she/her) is a NYC based writer, actor and accidental activist of Caribbean descent. She loves rewatching Avatar the Last Airbender, ordering takeout from different Black-owned restaurants and encouraging her loved ones to work through their traumas and enter their fullest state of being.

Meaghann Ande

Meaghann Ande is a nervous, loud, and snide nonprofiteer in the Pacific Northwest. Those who know her would describe her as a big personality that swings from Wednesday Addams' ennui to Leslie Knope's optimism and determination to save the world. She's built by and for stories and can't wait to share more of them with the world.

E. Jamar

E Jamar is a queer disabled freelance writer based in Milwaukee, WI. E often gets in trouble for pushing the status quo with their writing on ableism and trauma. When they're not writing, they can often be found contemplating disability justice, overdosing on caffeine, or hanging out with their partner and pug puppy named Acab.

CT Marie

CT Marie is a writer, director, producer, and actress based in New York. She wrote, produced, directed, and acted in "Rent Control," a web series that was an Official Selection of T.O. Webfest 2020 and the Winner of the "I Heart NY" Award, NYC Webfest 2020.

Acknowledgments

Amir Ali Said, my son, best friend, and Superchamp Books co-founder, As always, thank you for your friendship, knowledge, courage, and curiosity. We expanded Superchamp Books in a big way, and in making that possible, you surpassed all of my expectations. Also, an extra thanks for facilitating so many different tasks in the final hour, especially while I was away on book leave. I love you, Son, Alhumdulillah!

I would like to thank all of the writers who were published in this edition of *Dating & Sex: The Theory of Mutual Self-Destruction*:
Kyra Wolfe, Allyson Darling, Jenelle Parish, Jeana Jorgensen, Molly Godfrey Shane Thomas, Almaz Ohene, Melissa Gabso, Catherine Renton, Douglas Moser, Becca Beberaggi, Stephanie Parent, Hattie Gladwell, Blake Turck, Joe Duncan, Elena Fernández Collins, Lisa Levy, Marcus K. Dowling, D. Anne Tolentino, Alexandra Hogan Danielle Chelosky, Vonnnie Wright, Jennifer Greenberg, Suzannah Weiss, Carolyn Busa, June Moon, Rachel Davies, Mike McClelland, Aitza Burgess, Jeana Jorgensen, Stephanie Conway, Wil Williams, Gina Tonic, Shayna Conde, Meaghann Ande, Emily E. Jamar, and CT Marie.

This book took a lot of careful planning and required the support in various forms from a number of different people (I thank you all!), but there are some people I am compelled to single out here: Géraldine, Je te remercie pour tout ! mais surtout ta comprehension, ton soutien et ta purée. Christophe, merci frère, comme d'habitude. Sibel, thank you for checking in and helping to keep me on point. Hannah (UK), what a suprise, right? Thank you for being there to help me cut through all the long work days.

—Said

About the Series Creator & Editor

Amir Said (*Said*) is the co-founder of Superchamp Books and the creator and series editor of *Dating & Sex: The Theory of Mutual Self-Destruction*. He is a writer, musician, and publisher from Brooklyn, New York, now living in Paris, France. Said is also the creator and editor-in-chief of *Best Damn Writing magazine*, the creator and series editor of the *Best Damn Writing* book anthology series, and the creator and series editor of *Samir Cinema: The Journal of Modern Film, Television, and Streaming*.

Said has written a number of books including *The Beat Tips Manual*, *Ghetto Brother* (co-written with Benjy Melendez), *Medium Speed in the City Called Paris (Poetry)*, and *The Truth About New York*. His new book, *The Art of Sampling, 3rd Edition*, will be published in the spring of 2021.